You're the Top: Cole Porter in the 1930s

Cole Porter Centennial Collection

Indianapolis:
Indiana Historical Society
1992

©1992 Indiana Historical Society
©The Cole Porter Musical and Literary Property Trusts
(Porter biography)

All rights reserved. No part of this book may be reproduced or transmitted in any form or by any means, electronic or mechanical, including photocopying, recording, or by any information storage and retrieval system, without permission in writing from the publishers.

Printed in the United States of America

Contents

Cole Porter   1

The Songs   17

The Principal Performers   71

Performers   96

Discography   98

Bibliography   105

Credits   106

The Producers   107

The Yale Collection of Historical Sound Recordings   108

Music class at East Main Street grade school in Peru, Indiana, 1899, just two years before Porter composed "Song of the Birds."

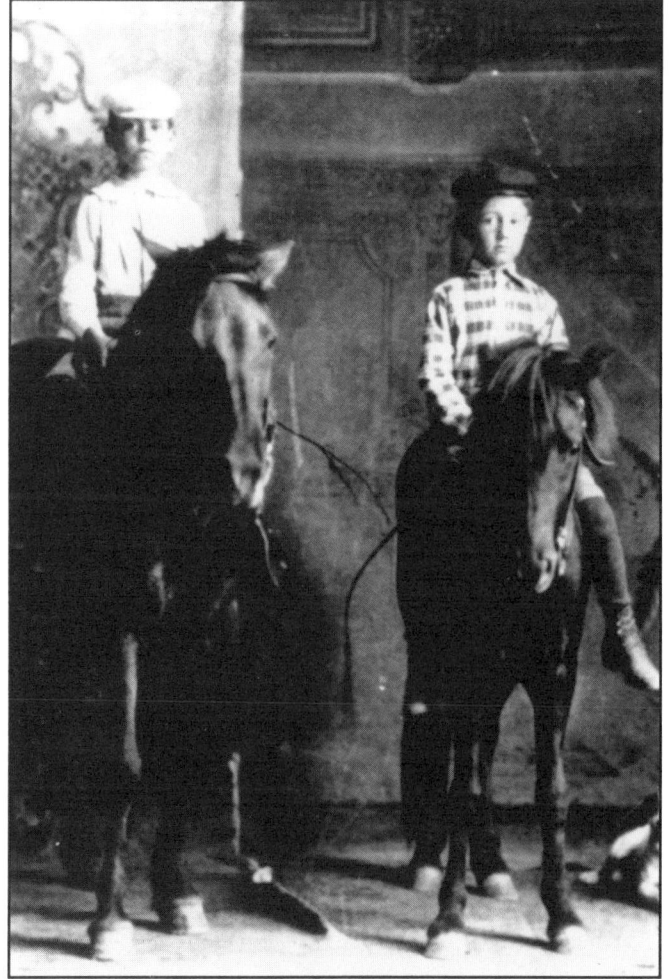

Porter (left) was given his own pony at age six. He is pictured here with his cousin, J. O. Cole, in the late 1890s.

Cole Porter

By Robert Kimball

The Roaring Twenties were over. The Jazz Age had come to a tumultuous close with the Stock Market Crash of October 1929. The last night of the decade offered parties galore, Prohibition raids, madcap revelry in New York's Times Square, and the customary predictions from government leaders of better times ahead. Treasury Secretary Andrew W. Mellon offered that "the nation will make steady progress during 1930." Commerce Secretary Robert P. Lamont projected "over the long run, a continuance of prosperity and progress." Even badly battered Wall Street was moderately bullish for 1930.

Few could have foreseen how much grief, anguish, and social dislocation would be wrought by the Great Depression that had just begun. Newspapers were filled with ads for January "fur and frock" clearance sales. Cruise lines promised "days of relaxation free from Northern chill."

On the New Year's Eve that preceded the new decade, all the Broadway musicals had been sold out. Five days later, in a column titled "Words and Music on 42nd St.," the *New York Times* saluted Broadway's man of the hour, composer of two of the three largest-grossing shows on the Great White Way:

> In that part of the acetylene district between Seventh and Eighth Avenues, where Forty-Second Street flows brightly toward the sea, the tireless statisticians of the theatre have been quick to discover two musical shows bearing the imprimatur of a single composer. At the Selwyn Theatre . . . is "Wake Up and Dream." At the Lyric is "Fifty Million Frenchmen." And somewhere about the premises of each is a placard bursting to say that the words and music in question leap light-footed from Cole Porter—the Mr. Porter who never wrote a mammy song, who never even whiled away an idle hour in wheedling thoughts of Dixie out of his bored piano.

That celebrated figure was to become Broadway's leading minstrel in the years between the Crash and the Second World War. Born in Peru, Indiana, on 9 June 1891, Cole Porter was the son of Kate Cole and Samuel Fenwick Porter. Two earlier children, Louis and Rachel, had died in infancy before his birth. He received his formal education at Worcester Academy in Massachusetts (1905–1909), Yale College (1909–13), Harvard Law and Music schools (1913–16), and the Schola Cantorum in Paris (1920–21). His musical education, one of the most extensive received by an American theater composer, began with his mother, who introduced him to the piano and violin at an early age. Young Cole's earliest attempts at composition produced such precocious concoctions as the "Song of the Birds" in 1901 and a year later, "The Bob-o-Link Waltz."

His appetite for lyric writing was whetted by his pharmacist father's avid interest in classical languages and nineteenth-century romantic poetry, both of which Cole pursued in prep school and college. At Yale he wrote two of the school's most famous football songs, "Bull Dog" and "Bingo, Eli Yale." His Yale Glee Club specialties and the musical comedy scores he wrote for the initiation plays (*Cora*, 1911 and *The Pot of Gold*, 1912) at his fraternity, Delta Kappa Epsilon, and for the "smokers" of the Yale Dramatic Association (*And the Villain Still Pursued Her*, 1912; *The Kaleidoscope*, 1913; and *Paranoia*, 1914) were fondly recalled by his contemporaries and are still valued for their suave, audacious lyrics and captivating music. He was also a gifted parodist and singer-pianist of such imposing talent that many of his college friends thought he had all the makings of a star vaudevillian.

Yet, for all his precocity and skill, Cole was dogged by a series of career disappointments that delayed his rise to the top of his profession until the late 1920s. His first Broadway musical—which came along at the same time as the effervescent offerings of George M. Cohan and Irving Berlin and the intimate Princess Theater shows of Guy Bolton, P. G. Wodehouse, and Jerome Kern—was the Anglophilic comic opera *See America First* (1916). This misguided attempt to Gilbert and Sullivanize the American musical by intermingling British peers and Indian maidens in an Arizona mesa lasted for just fifteen performances, although one of its numbers, "I've a Shooting Box in Scotland," became the first Porter song to be recorded commercially, by Joseph C. Smith and his Orchestra.

In June 1917 Porter sailed for Europe to work with the Duryea Relief Organization. Within a few months he had enlisted in the French Foreign Legion. Later in the war he was attached to the American Embassy in Paris where, on 30 January 1918, at a wedding breakfast in the Ritz Hotel for

Ethel Harriman and Henry Russell, he met the exquisite Linda Lee Thomas. Linda was an elegant divorcée whom Bernard Berenson once succinctly described as "a great beauty with great brains." She and Cole fell in love and were married in Paris on 18 December 1919.

From World War I until the late 1920s the Porters lived primarily overseas, mostly in Paris at 13 rue Monsieur, and at several palazzi in Venice, notably the Rezzonico. In Europe Cole gained a perspective—similar in many ways to that of the "lost generation" of literary exiles—that set him apart from the other great creators of the American musical theater. Cole's early passion for Alfred Tennyson, Robert Browning, and Algernon Swinburne was mated to a familiarity with nineteenth-century art songs and a knowledge of counterpoint, harmony, and orchestration that he sharpened during his studies at the Schola Cantorum in Paris with Vincent d'Indy and other teachers. He absorbed the innovations of Igor Stravinsky, the Gallic spirit of Darius Milhaud and Francis Poulenc, and American jazz. His ballet score—the satiric, jazz-tinged *Within the Quota* (1923), performed with success in Europe and the United States by the Swedish Ballet—predates George Gershwin's *Rhapsody in Blue* by several months.

Porter's travels, his endless quest for new places and fresh experiences, heightened his art and strengthened his individual voice. His years as a "playboy expatriate," when many people thought he was doing little but giving and going to parties, afforded him both the distance and the stimulation to develop his distinctive style. Encouraged by his wife, he remained steadfastly absorbed in his work, even against a fabulous, almost unreal backdrop of treasure hunts, beach parties, fashionable outings, and costume balls.

Still, his career as a theater composer foundered. While his songs were presented in such revues as *Hitchy-Koo of 1919*, *Mayfair and Montmartre* (1922), *Hitchy-Koo of 1922*, and *Greenwich Village Follies of 1924*, the response to his work was not encouraging, and he very nearly abandoned songwriting.

The creative doldrums and the years of frustration, after *See America First* failed, finally ended when Monty Woolley asked his friend Cole to submit songs for a Yale Dramat Christmas show in 1925. A visit to Venice by Fannie Brice in 1927 inspired Porter to write some numbers for her, including "Weren't We Fools?," which she sang at New York's Palace Theater. It was one of many songs that were composed for friends and performed at private parties; lamentably, only a few of these survive.

Then, in 1927, "I'm in Love Again," which had been dropped from the *Greenwich Village Follies of 1924*, became a favorite of bandleaders after they heard it at Bricktop's in Paris. Soon Paul Whiteman's recording made it a major success. But the most memorable assistance came from Irving Berlin, who, along with Noël Coward, was Porter's closest friend among theater composers and a great admirer of Porter's work. "I used to tell Cole," Berlin told this writer in the early 1970s, "that he should not try to write like anyone else. You know he was so clever he could imitate me or others whose work he liked. But again and again I told him, 'Be yourself!'"

In 1927 Berlin suggested to producer E. Ray Goetz, his brother-in-law from his first marriage, that Goetz find Porter on the Lido in Venice and persuade him to write some American songs with a French flavor for Goetz's new show. (Porter later said he fell on Goetz "like an over-eager puppy.") The result was Porter's first big hit, *Paris*, which premiered at Berlin's Music Box Theater on Broadway in 1928 with the great Gallic charmer Irene Bordoni—Mrs. Goetz—in a starring role. *Paris* was, in Porter's own words, "an instant smash. I was a musical-comedy writer in demand—and I was never in the doldrums after 1928." One song from the show, the amorously frank "Let's Do It, Let's Fall in Love," firmly established his reputation in the front ranks of theater composers.

By the end of the 1920s Porter had come into his own. As post–World War I energy turned to frenzy, stock speculations went sour, and the widespread belief that Utopia had a price tag was discredited by the Crash of 1929 and the Great Depression, Porter's witty lyrics and his suave, pulsating melodies became a heady tonic for a disillusioned age. His own world-weariness, shaped in part by the knowledge that his considerable wealth had not guaranteed either happiness or escape from boredom, was increasingly shared by others less affluent. He wrote tellingly of the pain and evanescence of emotional relationships. He gently mocked propriety and said that few things were simple or lasting or free from ambiguity. When America was in the depths of the depression in the 1930s—the decade of the songs in this collection—his was a message of civilized cheer. He told his audiences that they, like the Colosseum, the Louvre Museum, a Shakespeare sonnet, and Mickey Mouse, were simply, "the top." It was Porter's greatest, most productive decade, and he became one of its indispensable voices.

The thirties began with two Cole Porter shows running on Broadway. The New York production of the Charles Cochran revue, *Wake Up and Dream*, which bowed in London in March 1929, opened in December 1929 and turned out to be the last musical to open in Gotham in the 1920s. And *Fifty Million Frenchmen* was the first book show of Porter's maturity for which he furnished all the music and lyrics. Ostensibly a celebration of life in Paris, it was also a nimble, tuneful satire on American values in the Jazz Age. It ran out the 1929-30 season and was one of that theatrical year's biggest triumphs.

The cast of a Yale touring musical, circa 1915; Porter and Monty Woolley are seated on the floor.

Porter at age 18.

The Yale Whiffenpoofs in 1913; Porter is second from the right.

A charcoal portrait of Porter, dated 3 March 1919, by English artist Wilfrid de Glehn.

The New Yorkers (1930)

A few months after *Frenchmen* closed, Porter was back on Broadway with *The New Yorkers*, which opened 8 December 1930. As they had been in *Frenchmen*, Porter's colleagues were librettist Herbert Fields, director Monty Woolley, and producer E. Ray Goetz. This time Goetz took over the cavernous two thousand-seat Broadway Theater and for fourteen consecutive weeks (13 December 1930–14 March 1931), *The New Yorkers* was the Great White Way's highest-grossing show, reaching and even surpassing $50,000 in some weeks. A rather loosely structured offering (it was billed as "a sociological musical satire"), inspired by *The New Yorker* cartoons of Peter Arno, it boasted a large, stellar cast including Frances Williams, Charles King, Hope Williams, Ann Pennington, Richard Carle, Marie Cahill, Oscar Ragland, the Fred Waring Orchestra, and the comedy team of Lou Clayton, Eddie Jackson, and Jimmy Durante.

"One of the merriest, maddest musical comedies of recent issue skylarked into the Chestnut last night," warbled the *Philadelphia Public Record* of the show's out-of-town opening. In Newark it was lauded by the *Evening News* as "a whale of a show." "Quite the smartest . . . that has come this way during the current season," noted that city's *Star Eagle*.

In New York the show was hosannaed in the *Herald-Tribune* by Percy Hammond, who proclaimed it "a cold, sophisticated, ornamental and extravagant hit." Robert Garland saluted it in the *New York Telegram* as "chipper and cheerful and ever so engaging. . . . It's as obvious as an automat, as glittering as the Chrysler Tower and as mad and muddled as the Manhattan from which it derives its name."

Porter's beguiling score included "Love for Sale," "Where Have You Been?," "Let's Fly Away," "I'm Getting Myself Ready for You," and "I Happen to Like New York." For several weeks it seemed as if *The New Yorkers* might run through the season, but the economic downturn of the ever-worsening depression prematurely shuttered many theatrical offerings in the spring of 1931, including this lavish harlequinade that needed to gross nearly $40,000 per week to meet its huge expenses.

In 1931, after a tour of the Orient, Porter composed the score for a musical titled *Star Dust*. The presenter, once again, was to be Goetz, and Fields was to write the book. The star was to be Peggy Wood. But the show was never produced. Porter told one of his biographers, Richard Hubler (*The Cole Porter Story*, 1965), that the project was abandoned because a large tobacco company, which was going to put up the money, backed out when an extra tax was levied on cigarettes. The score would have included "I Worship You," which had been dropped from *Fifty Million Frenchmen*, and "But He Never Says He Loves Me," which was later retitled "The Physician" and put into *Nymph Errant* (1933). Three numbers intended for *Star Dust* later appeared in *Gay Divorce* (1932): "I've Got You on My Mind," "Mister and Missus Fitch," and "I Still Love the Red, White and Blue." *Star Dust*'s most famous casualty was "I Get a Kick Out of You," which, revised, was introduced in *Anything Goes* (1934).

Gay Divorce (1932)

Porter returned to Broadway in the fall of 1932 with *Gay Divorce*, the first show in which Fred Astaire appeared without his equally famous sister Adele. (She retired from the stage after starring in *The Band Wagon* [1931] to marry Lord Charles Cavendish.) In addition to Astaire, the cast featured Claire Luce, Luella Gear, Betty Starbuck, Erik Rhodes, Eric Blore, and G. P. Huntley, Jr. There were tryout problems: the book had to be revised substantially prior to the New York premiere at the Ethel Barrymore Theater on 29 November 1932. But ultimately Porter fashioned one of his most urbane and elegant scores. Soon after the opening, "Night and Day," arguably Porter's most famous song and fourteen years later the title of his screen biography, became the best-selling song in America.

There was a successful London production in 1933, for which Porter wrote three new songs, and a 1934 film version titled *The Gay Divorcée*, which starred Astaire and Ginger Rogers. It included only one song—"Night and Day"—from the 1932 Broadway production.

After *Gay Divorce* Porter contemplated a number of projects. For a time he worked on a musical with the well-known playwright Frederick Lonsdale. In December 1932 the *New York Herald-Tribune* reported that he was writing songs for a new revue titled *Très Bien*, to be produced by Courtney Burr. A few months later (May 1933) Dwight Deere Wiman and Tom Weatherly, the producers of *Gay Divorce*, were mentioned in several stories as conceiving a show that was to star Jack Haley and Fred Allen. The book was to be by Bertram Robinson and Daniel Kussell; Howard Lindsay would direct. "The name of the offering is 'Tu Hu,'" cited the *New York Times*, which added that "unless someone is joking pretty earnestly its locale is China." Nothing came of any of these ventures, and no songs for any of them survive.

Nymph Errant (1933)

Early in 1933 English producer Charles Cochran read a book called *Nymph Errant* by James Laver, a curator and expert on costumes at the Victoria and Albert Museum in London. The book was about the mostly amorous exploits of a

Linda, by Edward Steichen, in the 1920s.

Cole and Linda Porter's living room at 13 rue Monsieur, Paris, where they lived in the 1920s.

young girl, fresh from finishing school, who sets out to lose her virginity and see the world. Cochran enjoyed the book so much that he engaged Romney Brent to adapt it for the stage; Porter was persuaded to furnish the score. Gertrude Lawrence, who had introduced two Porter songs in the 1929 film, *The Battle of Paris*, and whose "quality of dramatic radiance" Cochran considered unique, was signed for the starring role of Evangeline. Joining her in the cast were Iris Ashley, Doris Carson, Walter Crisham, Austin Trevor, David Burns, and Elisabeth Welch. Agnes de Mille provided the choreography, her first major assignment for the stage.

Although *Nymph Errant* enjoyed a glittering London premiere, it mustered a modest run of only 154 performances and was not presented in America until 1982. Years after the show's opening, Porter, who had described the score as the best he had ever written, lamented that "a Hollywood motion-picture company, Fox, later Twentieth Century-Fox, bought it and, naturally, never produced it."

On 21 January 1934 an article in the *Indianapolis Star* noted that Porter was working on a musical for Gilbert Miller. It was based on a play called *The Spell* by Lili Hatvany and was known variously as *Yours*, *Ever Yours*, and *Once Upon a Time*. Guy Bolton tried his hand at the libretto, a version of which survives, but the enterprise was abandoned without a production. One of its songs, "When Love Comes Your Way," also dropped from *Nymph Errant*, later found its way into *Jubilee* (1935).

Anything Goes (1934)

And then came *Anything Goes*, which musical theater historian Miles Kreuger, in his liner notes for John McGlinn's complete recording of the score for EMI, described as "the bright and cheerful embodiment of Roosevelt recovery." It was the brainchild of producer Vinton Freedley who, with his partner Alex Aarons, had given New York and London a number of the smartest offerings of the 1920s by George and Ira Gershwin, as well as some works by Richard Rodgers and Lorenz Hart.

When the Gershwins' *Pardon My English* failed in 1933, the Freedley-Aarons team dissolved, and Freedley fled his creditors by taking a fruit boat to Panama. While lazing the days away fishing near Tobago, he conceived a show that would be about characters on a ship bound for England. Freedley decided it should be as intimate as the Princess Theater shows of the 1910s and called on Bolton, Wodehouse, and Porter to make his dream a reality. Before he even had book in hand, he decided that the stars should be the team of William Gaxton and Victor Moore and the clarion-voiced Ethel Merman, who had made her Broadway debut in Freedley and Aarons's *Girl Crazy*.

The three writers were living in Europe, so Freedley set sail to confer with them. As it turned out, Bolton was in England and would not travel to Paris, Wodehouse was on the French Riviera and did not want to go to London, and Porter, whose main residence was in Paris, was faltboating down the Rhine. Somehow, Freedley corralled the trio to the French coastal town of Le Touquet-Paris Plage and began work.

By mid-August 1934, a script was dispatched to Freedley in New York, and on 16 August Porter stepped off the luxury liner *Ile de France* in New York, completed score in hand. Three weeks later the Bolton Wodehouse script, which had the threat of an explosion at sea as part of its denouement, had to be jettisoned because the S.S. *Morro Castle* burst into flames off Asbury Park, New Jersey, killing over one hundred people. When Bolton and Wodehouse could not come quickly to New York to make the necessary repairs, Freedley engaged Howard Lindsay and Russel Crouse to craft a largely new libretto. On 5 November 1934 *Anything Goes* opened triumphantly in Boston. Three weeks later it became the toast of Broadway. Porter called it "the most famous show I was associated with." It ran for 420 performances, played in London, was filmed twice, and has been revived and recorded many times since. It has become almost synonymous with the decade in which it was born.

Adios, Argentina (1934–35) and Jubilee (1935)

After the spectacular launch of *Anything Goes*, Porter signed a contract with Twentieth Century-Fox to provide songs for a film tentatively titled *Adios, Argentina*. The screenplay—by Allen Rivkin and the film's producer, Lou Brock—was about an orphan girl who had inherited a big cattle spread in Texas, and how she shipped her four polo-playing cowboy tutors East to challenge the winner of a polo match between the United States and Argentina teams. Porter wrote and recorded six numbers for the film, one of which has a fascinating story. There was a point in the script where the cowhands were supposed to sing of their loneliness for life back on the ranch. With the help of a title and several words and phrases from a poem written by Montana traffic engineer Robert Fletcher, Porter composed "Don't Fence Me In." When *Adios, Argentina* was abandoned, the song languished in obscurity for nearly ten years before it was rescued from the Warner Bros. Music files and sung by Roy Rogers in the 1944 film *Hollywood Canteen*.

Less than a week after recording the songs for *Adios, Argentina*, Cole, joined by Linda Porter, Moss Hart, Monty Woolley, the Porters' friend Howard Sturges, and travel writer William Powell, embarked on the S.S. *Franconia* of the Cunard White Star Line for a 37,000-mile Southern

Linda Porter and Howard Sturges on the boardwalk in Atlantic City, New Jersey, in 1924.

Jack Wilson, Noël Coward, and Porter on the Lido in Venice in 1926. Elsa Maxwell dubbed Noël and Cole, "Noëly and Coley."

Porter on the Lido, Venice, in the mid-1920s, in bathing cap and pearls.

Hemisphere cruise around the world. They sailed from New York in the early hours of 12 January 1935 and returned on 31 May. When they disembarked, Porter and Hart brought with them the score and book for their new musical *Jubilee*. Part musical comedy, part operetta, and part masquerade, *Jubilee* chronicled a mythical royal family, its escape from its regal responsibilities, and its adventures disguised as commoners. For *Jubilee*, Porter fashioned one of the most ambitious and richly varied scores of his career.

After a notable Boston tryout, *Jubilee* opened at New York's Imperial Theater on 12 October 1935 (two days after the premiere of *Porgy and Bess*) to generally favorable notices. Despite fires, thefts, accidents, and cast squabbles, the show was headed for what looked to be a lengthy engagement. However, the departure for Hollywood of the star, Mary Boland, from the cast early in 1936 sent box-office receipts plummeting, closing the production after 169 performances. Years later, three of *Jubilee*'s songs ("Begin the Beguine," "Why Shouldn't I?," and "Just One of Those Things") came to be considered among Porter's finest work. The entire score awaits rediscovery.

Born to Dance (1936)

In late 1935, after a Bermuda vacation, the Porters traveled to Hollywood where they rented the Richard Barthelmess house while Cole awaited word from MGM on the nature of his assignment. While Linda disliked the social atmosphere that surrounded the film colony, Cole went Hollywood, in the words of columnist Dorothy Kilgallen, "quickly and completely." "When I first came out here," he told her in a 1936 *New York Evening Journal* interview, "they told me 'You'll be so bored you'll die; nobody talks about anything but pictures.' After I was here a week, I discovered I didn't want to talk about anything else myself."

The first three months there was a time of utter confusion. Finally, authors Jack McGowan and Sid Silvers came up with an idea: a nautical escapade about sailors and a lonely hearts club. Its working title was *Great Guns*. Porter finished most of the songs between March and May, and on 3 June he played his numbers for Louis B. Mayer and Irving Thalberg. They liked it so much they asked him to write another score for MGM, raising his fee from $75,000 to $100,000.

Renamed *Born to Dance*, it starred James Stewart and Eleanor Powell (in the first of her three MGM films with Porter scores) and featured Virginia Bruce, Una Merkel, Frances Langford, and Buddy Ebsen. Opening in early December 1936 at New York's Capitol Theater, *Born to Dance* won widespread critical and public acceptance and boasted two of Porter's best songs—"Easy to Love" and "I've Got You under My Skin." It also initiated Porter's practice of writing one film score and one stage score per year, a pattern he tried to follow whenever he could.

Red, Hot and Blue! (1936)

Cole's next stage work, *Red, Hot and Blue!*, written mostly in the summer of 1936, was anything but trouble-free, even though it was conceived by the team that wrote and produced *Anything Goes*. In early 1935 Vinton Freedley went to Hollywood to convince producer Samuel Goldwyn to temporarily release Eddie Cantor from his contract. On 6 February 1935 Freedley announced that he had signed Cantor to star in a new, untitled Broadway musical to be written by Howard Lindsay and Russel Crouse with music and lyrics by Cole Porter, who was on his world cruise at the time. In the spring of 1935 Freedley signed Ethel Merman and waited for Cantor to become available. The show was planned for the fall of 1935, but late that year Cantor withdrew from the project.

Along the road to production, a number of artists including Sid Silvers, Willie and Eugene Howard, Jack Benny, William Gaxton, and Bert Lahr were rumored to be in the show. By June 1936 Freedley had signed Bob Hope for what was to be his last Broadway show. After a last try to obtain the services of Willie Howard, Freedley also engaged Jimmy Durante, who had been vacationing in Capri.

In May of 1936 the show's title was *But Millions*, soon to become *—But Millions $* and then *Wait for Baby*. In late July 1936 it became *Red, Hot and Blue!*, and Porter wrote a title song. The wacky story, a kind of throwback to the plot of the Gershwins' *Of Thee I Sing* (1931), was about a national lottery to find a girl who had sat on a waffle iron when she was four. Theater histories recall the show for its battle between Merman's and Durante's agents over who would receive top billing. It was Porter who came up with the ingenious solution of crisscrossing the names of Durante and Merman over the show's title and then changing the position of their names every two weeks. (*See p. 50*.)

There were book problems during the tryouts in Boston and New Haven; the show was too long. While Porter rallied to the emergency by composing "Down in the Depths (on the 90th Floor)" in two days to replace "Goodbye, Little Dream, Goodbye," he became frustrated and left the production for several days before heeding an SOS from Freedley to return.

At the New York opening (Alvin Theater, 29 October 1936), *Red, Hot and Blue!* drew moderately favorable notices. "Very merry," said John Mason Brown in the *New York Post*. "Far from sensational," noted Julius Cort in the *New York Journal of Commerce*. Brooks Atkinson's measured view in the *New York Times* most closely reflected the critical consensus: "If *Anything Goes* is your standard, be prepared for a fall off in book coherence." After a modest run of 183 performances, there was a brief tour.

What was most significant about the show for Porter was his realization, publicly expressed, that his songs had been reaching too limited an audience to ensure substantial runs for the shows from which they came. In an interview Porter said that "sophisticated allusions are good for about six weeks. Futile as presenting Sophocles in the original Greek. Sophisticated lyrics are more fun but only for myself and about eighteen other people, all of whom are first-nighters anyway. Polished, urbane, and adult playwriting in the musical field is strictly a creative luxury."

As if to prove his thesis, soon after opening night Porter deleted the suave ballad "You're a Bad Influence on Me," which offered such lines as "Your ev'ry move fills me with fright, But I beg you, dear, come up tonight" and "I wish you'd cease singeing my wings, But before you do take off your things," and replaced it with the mock hillbilly ditty, "The Ozarks Are Callin' Me Home."

ROSALIE (1937)

Porter's next assignment from MGM was the film *Rosalie*, which was loosely based on the Broadway stage musical of 1928. He wrote most of its songs in the spring and early summer of 1937. *Rosalie* starred Eleanor Powell, Nelson Eddy, Frank Morgan, Edna May Oliver, Ilona Massey, and the young singer-comedian Ray Bolger. It opened on 20 December 1937 and proved to be a large, costly, only intermittently lively extravaganza. Wanda Hale wrote in the *New York Daily News*, "While *Rosalie* offers a certain amount of entertainment and amusement in Eddy's singing, Powell's dancing, Ray Bolger's and Frank Morgan's comedy, and Cole Porter's already popular tunes and songs, Metro [MGM] fumbled this adaptation of Florenz Ziegfeld's beautiful show of a decade ago." Margaret Tazelaar of the *New York Herald-Tribune* described it as "a mythical kingdom bore," while the *New York Times* saw it as "one of the most pretentious demonstrations of sheer mass and weight since the last Navy Games."

Yet *Rosalie* is still remembered for introducing one of Porter's masterpieces, "In the Still of the Night," the buoyant "I've a Strange New Rhythm in My Heart," and another entry in Porter's deliberately popular vein, "Rosalie," a song he never liked. In a 1946 letter to bandleader Paul Whiteman, Porter recalled, "When the song became a hit, I saw Irving Berlin and he congratulated me on it. I said to him, 'Thanks a lot but I wrote that song in hate and I still hate it.' To which Irving replied, 'Listen, kid, take my advice, never hate a song that has sold a half-million copies.'"

While still in Europe, after completing the songs for *Rosalie*, Porter went with friends Howard Sturges and Ed Tauch on a sojourn from the Dolomites to Scandinavia. He was asked by E. Ray Goetz to write two songs for a René Clair film titled *The Laugh of the Town*. Porter completed "It All Belongs to You" and "Don't Let It Get You Down" during August 1937 and sent them to Clair, but only the former was used. The film, retitled *Break the News* and released in 1938, starred Maurice Chevalier, Jack Buchanan, and June Knight.

On 26 September 1937, a story in the *New York Herald-Tribune* announced that Vinton Freedley was planning to present a musical, *Greek to You*, based on an "original talking motion picture comedy" by William Jordan Rapp and Lowell Brentano. It was to star Clifton Webb, and the book was to be written by Howard Lindsay and Russel Crouse, with songs by Porter. An outline of the book survives, but the project was never finished. When Porter returned from his European vacation in early October 1937, Lindsay and Crouse were still deeply involved in completing *Hooray for What?* (music by Harold Arlen, lyrics by E. Y. Harburg), a musical that opened at the Winter Garden on 1 December 1937. Nothing more about *Greek to You* is known to have been written until a 27 June 1938 article in the *New York Herald-Tribune* announced that Freedley had abandoned it. One number that survived—"Most Gentlemen Don't Like Love"—ended up in the score for *Leave It to Me* (1938).

The Accident (1937)

Several days after he returned to the States, Porter accepted a weekend invitation to join friends at the home of Countess Edith di Zoppola (the former Edith Mortimer) on Long Island. On 24 October he went riding early in the morning at the Piping Rock Club in Locust Valley. As Porter recalled: "I took my horse up a mildly steep hill. It was wet and slippery. My horse shied at some bushes—I did not pull back on the reins as some insisted afterward—and he reared and fell on me. I woke up in a local hospital with both legs broken in compound fractures, an important nerve nearly cut in two. From then on I spent months under sedatives. Through the years I underwent thirty-three bone operations under the jurisdiction of John J. Moorhead, the best bone surgeon we could find."

As Porter recuperated, he heeded the advice of Dr. Moorhead: "Work! Work! as you've never worked before." "I think it saved my mind as well as my legs," Porter later recalled. "My semi-doped brain seemed to be buzzing with tunes. To keep at my writing, I had my piano raised on wooden blocks and sat at it in a wheelchair."

Clifford Sabrey, Howard Sturges, Monty Woolley, and Porter in New Zealand, one stop on a 1935 'round-the-world cruise.

In port at Madagascar in 1935. Porter is on mat (front left).

YOU'RE THE TOP: COLE PORTER IN THE 1930S

Porter at the piano, circa 1940.

Porter being carried to the Broadway opening of Noël Coward's Set to Music *in 1939.*

You Never Know (1938)

At the entreaty of the Shuberts and Clifton Webb, who had appeared in Porter's first Broadway musical, *See America First*, Porter agreed to write the score for *You Never Know*, an adaptation of the light comedy *By Candlelight*. By February 1938 most of the songs were completed. In addition to Webb, the cast starred Lupe Velez and Libby Holman. *You Never Know* began its tryouts at the Shubert Theater in New Haven on 3 March 1938 and, over the next few months of an extended road tour, was transformed from a relatively intimate musical comedy into a large-scale, rather ponderous Shubert show. It bowed at the Winter Garden on 21 September 1938 and closed after seventy-eight performances. Porter aptly characterized it as an "immense flop." Yet one standard emerged, "At Long Last Love."

Leave It to Me (1938)

That spring Porter began writing the score for Sam and Bella Spewack's adaptation of their play *Clear All Wires*, which poked fun at United States diplomacy and communism. Titled *Leave It to Me*, it starred Tamara, Sophie Tucker, William Gaxton, and Victor Moore. June Knight was also cast, but she had to be replaced when she ran off and married a Texas millionaire. "An agent called me," Porter later recalled, "and said he had a client who might fit the role. I asked him up and he appeared, leading a dreary little girl who appeared to be the last word in scared dowdiness. My pianist played and she sang. . . . It was the finest audition I have ever heard. . . . A star was born named Mary Martin. Her voice and charm have been national assets ever since."

The song Martin made famous was, of course, "My Heart Belongs to Daddy." Also delightful were "Most Gentlemen Don't Like Love," as put over by Sophie Tucker, and the bittersweet lament, "Get Out of Town," sung by Tamara. Among those making Broadway debuts in the chorus was Gene Kelly. After a tryout in New Haven and Boston, *Leave It to Me* opened at New York's Imperial Theater on 9 November 1938, presented by Vinton Freedley. It enjoyed a successful run of 307 performances. "A handsome carnival," Brooks Atkinson of the *New York Times* termed it. "A mad and delectable affair," wrote John Mason Brown of the *New York Post*. "One of Cole Porter's choicest scores," stated Richard Watts, Jr., in the *New York Herald-Tribune*.

Broadway Melody of 1940 (1939)

The Porters spent Christmas of 1938 in Cartagena, Colombia. In the spring of 1939, Cole, his friend Ray Kelly, and his valet Paul Sylvain, journeyed to Machu Picchu in the Peruvian Andes, a difficult trip for someone in Porter's physical condition. When he returned to the Malibu Beach house he had rented from Richard Barthelmess, he began work on the score of what was to have been MGM's *Broadway Melody of 1939*. It paired Fred Astaire and Eleanor Powell, featured George Murphy, and is best remembered for some of its dance sequences and Porter's classic song "I Concentrate on You." The score was completed in the summer of 1939, but the film, retitled *Broadway Melody of 1940*, was not released until the following February.

Du Barry Was a Lady (1939)

By the end of the 1930s Porter was reaping a harvest of huge success for his score for *Du Barry Was a Lady*. It starred Ethel Merman and Bert Lahr, with Betty Grable, Benny Baker, Charles Walters, and Ronald Graham also in the cast. It was the last musical to open on Broadway during the decade, and, for Porter, its run of 408 performances made it his second biggest hit of the 1930s. *Du Barry* was a bright, bountiful, bawdy show that juxtaposed a contemporary New York night club and the court life of eighteenth-century France. With book by Herbert Fields and B. G. De Sylva, its story traces the Mickey Finn transformation of Bert Lahr, the club's washroom attendant, into a dreamland where he is King Louis XV and Ethel Merman, the night club's singing star, is Du Barry. The blending of disparate worlds, which Porter also accomplished later in *Kiss Me, Kate* and *Out of This World*, was cleverly realized in Porter's witty, ingenious score. Swing was embodied in a number such as "When Love Beckoned," while such dance forms as the gavotte, loure, and minuet evoked the spirit of eighteenth-century France.

1940–64

Porter continued his string of Broadway hits until early 1944. Such Gotham crowd pleasers as *Panama Hattie* (1940), *Let's Face It* (1941), *Something for the Boys* (1943), and *Mexican Hayride* (1944) provided theatergoers with cheerful, undemanding wartime diversions, while his run of film scores continued with *You'll Never Get Rich* (1941)—a particularly fine pairing of Fred Astaire and Rita Hayworth—and *Something to Shout About* (1943), one of the rare films of the period that avoided any mention of World War II.

After *Mexican Hayride*, it is commonly assumed that Porter went through a four-year dry spell that began with the 1944 revue *Seven Lively Arts* and continued through *Around the World in Eighty Days* (1946) and *The Pirate* (1948), a film

for Judy Garland and Gene Kelly. But it ended triumphantly with *Kiss Me, Kate* (1948), the first musical to win a Tony Award. *Kate* was followed by the ambitious, but markedly less successful *Out of This World*, which was buoyed by one of his most hilarious yet sublimely beautiful scores. Porter capped his Broadway career with two rather more conventional offerings, *Can-Can* (1953) and *Silk Stockings* (1955), which allowed him to return musically and lyrically to his beloved Paris. Then, with a pair of film scores, *High Society* (1956) and *Les Girls* (1957), and songs for the television production *Aladdin* (1958), his career ended.

The 1950s also brought a string of personal misfortunes. Cole's beloved mother, the great Kate, died in the summer of 1952; his wife Linda succumbed to emphysema in 1954; and his closest friend, Howard Sturges, passed away in 1955. In the spring of 1958 Cole's right leg was amputated. He finally lost the will to write after the amputation and died in Santa Monica, California, on 15 October 1964.

Of the many tributes he received at his death, none was more eloquent than the citation that accompanied his honorary degree from Yale University on 9 June 1960:

Cole Porter:

As an undergraduate, you first won acclaim for writing the words and music of two of Yale's perennial football songs. Since then you have achieved a reputation as a towering figure in the American musical theater. Master of the deft phrase, the delectable rhyme, the distinctive melody, you are, in your own words and in your own field, the top. . . . Your graceful, impudent, inimitable songs will be played and sung as long as footlights burn and curtains go up. . . .

Teddi King in the mid-1950s.

The Songs
By Richard M. Sudhalter

THE NEW YORKERS (1930)

I'm Getting Myself Ready for You
Emil Coleman and his Orchestra

The Great Depression was a year old and very much a fact of American life by 8 December 1930, when *The New Yorkers* opened at New York's Broadway Theater. Billed as a "sociological musical satire," it deftly matched the nation's mood: unsentimental, downbeat, a little cynical about nearly everything, particularly any notion of law and order. Even "I'm Getting Myself Ready for You," its most upbeat number, delivers a typical Porter sting: the singer pledges to modify his diet in preparation for matrimony. But rather than the expected proscriptions—pastries, rich sauces, chateaubriand, or vintage wines—it is eggs, onion soup, corned beef hash, and pork and beans. Such stuff may pose little threat to "building the perfect physique," but it is all too often a source of acute (and acrid) social embarrassment.

Emil Coleman's orchestra sets things out in appropriately cheery, rhythmic fashion, highlighted twice by an uncredited trumpet soloist whose phrasing is a bit reminiscent of Charlie Teagarden, kid brother of jazz trombonist Jack. The singer, also unbilled, sounds a lot like Smith Ballew, the handsome Texan who forged successive careers first as a contract vocalist for record companies, then as singing host of his own radio show, and finally as star of many minor western movies of the 1930s.

During the late 1920s and early 1930s, record companies customarily supplied their own vocalists for band dates. For a few years, until other bands started to follow the example established in the mid-1920s by Paul Whiteman and Bing Crosby, the labels' contract singers did very well indeed. Such performers as Harold "Scrappy" Lambert, Chick Bullock, Dick Robertson, and the aforementioned Ballew appear on thousands of recordings, by bands black and white, hot and sweet, immortal and forgettable. They brought good intonation, clarity of diction, and an ability to deliver the melodic line and lyrics of a song exactly as the composer had intended it.

Where Have You Been?
Teddi King

Once it had Teddi King under contract, RCA appears not to have been able to make up its collective mind what to do with her. There were records with hip, swinging big bands playing arrangements by Al Cohn; records with large, lush orchestras, usually under the direction of arranger George Siravo; even records backed by vocal groups that seemed to do little else but solemnly intone "doo-doo-*wah*" behind her.

Throughout it all, Teddi remained unflappably Teddi, forever a lady. But it deeply disturbed her. "I worked the big rooms, and was on network TV," she told *The New Yorker* jazz critic Whitney Balliett, "and the public became aware of my name. But it wasn't me. I was doing pop pap, and I was in musical despair. . . . I got very depressed and thought of quitting the business."

Even in the midst of her despair over how things were going at RCA, she managed to turn in performances such as this one, a gem introduced by Charles King and Hope Williams in *The New Yorkers*. Teddi's voice, with its purity and distinctive fast vibrato, somehow conjures visions of brilliant white sails scudding along atop a racing current on some glad-to-be-alive New England day.

There is a sense of wonder in her reading of the line, "When out of the blue you descended/And somehow ended ev'ry care." Listening to her here, it is easy to understand Teddi's explanation to Balliett that, "when I sing, I'm in a little shell. I feel as if I'm reciting a poem. If there is a person in the lyrics . . . I become that person. The lyrics direct my choice of notes. They take over, and I can just open my mouth and the sound follows."

The alto saxophone swooping gracefully in the background is played by longtime New York studio reedman Bernie Kaufman, a regular member of the orchestra on the Perry Como television show. "All I remember of those dates," Kaufman said recently, "is how beautifully she sang. A pure, lovely voice—and a lovely person. She was a treat to work with."

Lee Wiley, circa 1941, performing on NBC's Blue network, which later became ABC.

Let's Fly Away
Lee Wiley

His name appears in few books, but John De Vries has made a surprising amount of jazz history. It was De Vries, advertising artist and quondam lyricist, who went to see the *Ziegfeld Follies of 1936* at the Winter Garden Theater one night, picked up a sheet-music copy of its hit song in the lobby, and strolled a few blocks over to the Famous Door, on West 52nd Street, to show it to a couple of pals—pianist Joe Bushkin and trumpeter Bunny Berigan. Thus did "I Can't Get Started" fall into the hands of its best-known popularizer.

It was De Vries, too, who suggested to Bill Hill, owner of the prestigious Liberty Music shops, that he might record an album devoted to works of a single composer, featuring another friend of his, vocalist Lee Wiley, backed by a small jazz band. Hill was intrigued. In 1939 the concept of a one-composer album was unheard-of, innovative. His first shot was a set of Gershwin tunes; it sold well enough to make a Porter album possible.

"But make no mistake," said De Vries in a recent conversation. "Bill Hill was more than a little dismayed at the way the sessions were run. He was used to people like Bea Lillie, Ethel Merman—real pros. At our sessions—well, everybody was good and loaded. They were in it for kicks. Bottles everywhere. They didn't know it was going to be a historically important occasion. Lee just took off her shoes and sang. Bill was absolutely—well, he didn't know what to think. But he was into it, so we just went ahead."

Acetate "safeties" of the session, recently issued, reveal that Bunny Berigan, who plays trumpet obbligato to the Wiley vocal and solos passionately on "Let's Fly Away," emerged as a peacemaker at the sessions. "Lee could be difficult," said De Vries. "Bunny was a seasoned professional, the only one in the group, and he held it all together."

Some recent performances of "Let's Fly Away" have modernized the lyrics; but somehow the allusion to Roosevelt as a controversial figure (that, too, updated from the original "prohibition") or acknowledgment of Walter Winchell's power as a columnist greatly enhance the song's flavor.

I Happen to Like New York
Judy Garland

New York—its grandeur, diversity, elegance, gritty energy—seems forever able to tap into the passions of those composers and lyricists who elect to celebrate it in song. From Rodgers and Hart's 1925 "Manhattan" through Billy Joel's 1975 "New York State of Mind," songwriters have waxed emotional about the Big Apple.

Cole Porter was no exception. "The whole town is whistling and singing the big song hits in *The New Yorkers*," the *New York Evening Journal* commented on 23 December 1930. The story goes on to imply that Porter wrote this paean to the big city while on a ship en route to a Monte Carlo vacation, then cabled it to producer E. Ray Goetz. The lyric, perhaps, but no one in 1930, apparently, stopped to question how he had contrived to transmit the music. "I Happen to Like New York" was first listed in the official programs the week of 19 January 1931, so it seems likely that Porter mailed his lead sheet back to New York after he made port.

Judy Garland loved the song, and her performance here, recorded in London in 1960, is a revelation. Her voice cuts through all the orchestral and choral gift-wrapping like a ray of light, steady and intense. Somehow she creates intimacy amid all the hubbub, as if she were singing with just a pianist, for a small and attentive audience.

For Dave Lee, her pianist and arranger on the date, that's the way it always was with her. "You know, I've worked as musical director with many, many artists," said Lee recently. (He is now founder-director of JAZZ-FM, London's twenty-four-hour jazz radio station.) "Judy was quite the most professional I've ever worked with. On new arrangements—this one was no exception—she had me write down the entire orchestration like a script, or radio continuity part.

"She'd then memorize it, so she'd know, for example, when the drums would change from sticks to brushes, or when the strings should be muted, or when the trumpets played in cups. She'd say to me, 'You won't always be around, honey, and I don't want to be messed around by a band. I want to be able to turn to a conductor and say that at such-and-such a point the drummer should be doing this and that. That's what happens in this business, and you've got to know your own part very well.'"

Lee obviously relished his memories. "Look," he continued, "I worked with this woman for four years, sometimes five days a week. She was never late for a rehearsal. Never had off days, at least that I ever saw. All those stories about drink and drugs, about her being difficult when she was miserable—it might have been true at one time or another, but I never saw it. All I knew was that she was the best singer, best performer, hardest worker, most professional of them all.

"We did this date at EMI's big Abbey Road Studios, with Norrie Paramour conducting, and as usual Judy was there an hour early. We had a cup of coffee and went through everything, as we always did, just to make sure everything was fine and her voice was warmed up. She was such a perfectionist—and on these dates she was determined that it all be right.

"We had the best guys in town: Kenny Baker and Stan Roderick among the trumpets, Don Lusher and George Chisholm in the trombones. Kenny Clare on drums."

Libby Holman in 1930.

Lee paused. "One more thing: We did a show in Paris, an enormous success. She did all her encores, but it wasn't enough. They wanted more. So she went back out and did the whole second half of her program all over again. It ended up with her singing 'For Me and My Gal' with the Duke of Windsor and—who was it?—Yul Brynner, I think, joining in. All of them singing 'The bells are ringing, for me and my gal.' Believe me, if *that* doesn't move you, nothing ever will."

Love for Sale
Libby Holman

Controversy and scandal engulfed "Love for Sale" from the moment it was introduced. Porter told biographer Richard Hubler that he had dreamed it up one night during an evening walk in London, but the storm of criticism loosed by its opening night performance in New York belied such tranquil origins.

Witness Percy Hammond, writing in the *New York Herald-Tribune*: "A frightened vocalist, Miss Kathryn Crawford, sings a threnody entitled 'Love for Sale' in which she impersonates a lily of the gutters, vending her charms in trembling accents, accompanied by a trio of melancholy female crooners. When and if we ever get a censorship, I will give odds that it will frown upon such an honest thing."

Frown? It positively scowled. Charles Darnton, writing in the *New York World*, found the song "in the worst possible taste." Not unexpectedly, it was banned from performance on the radio. The show's producers, intimidated by even the prospect of such conflict, quickly caved in and (reportedly at the suggestion of Irving Berlin) moved the setting of "Love for Sale" uptown to the Cotton Club; prostitution, they seemed to be saying, was objectionable in (white) midtown but all right in (black) Harlem.

Even so craven a move had its beneficial outcome. In January 1931 Elisabeth Welch replaced Kathryn Crawford and quickly made "Love for Sale" her own, an early step in a long and distinguished career.

Libby Holman, no stranger to scandal herself, did very well with her own recording of what Porter later cited (along with "Begin the Beguine" and "Night and Day") as a favorite among his own songs. Her deficiencies as a singer—unreliable pitch, a tendency to swallow whole phrases—are only too manifest here; but somehow she manages to convince. The torch singer's blend of toughness and vulnerability that saw her through "Moanin' Low" and "Body and Soul" serves her equally well here.

Love for Sale
Ruby Braff and Ellis Larkins

John Hammond, whose role in the careers of, among others, Benny Goodman, Billie Holiday, and Count Basie has been often and well documented, also had much to do with turning the spotlight on Ruby Braff. As a producer for Vanguard Records, Hammond featured the twenty-seven-year-old Boston trumpeter in 1954 with a group led by trombonist Vic Dickenson, and when those two ten-inch LPs drew critical praise, he decided to go for broke and give the newcomer a date of his own.

"John wanted to record me with bass, drums, the usual stuff," Braff said recently. "I told him no—I'd done all that. 'Well,' he said, 'what do you *want* to do?' I told him that one of my very favorite records was of just Ella Fitzgerald with Ellis Larkins at the piano doing some Gershwin tunes. I said I'd love to do something with Ellis. Well, John said okay, and all the rest of his life he took credit for the idea."

Whoever thought of it, the result was superb. Larkins, elegant and conservatory-precise, proved a perfect foil for Braff's passionately melodic approach to his horn. They recorded in an old Masonic temple in Brooklyn. "What a wonderful sound—high ceilings, and a wonderful warmth," said Braff. "And just one microphone hanging there. Ellis was at the very top of his artistry. As I remember it, we got just about everything in one take. Listening now, it all has that fresh-minted quality to it. Of course, that's how everything seemed to me back then. Just a delight."

Let's Step Out (added to *Fifty Million Frenchmen* in March 1930)
Mister Tram Associates

Edmund Anderson seems to be one of those people fortunate enough to have been in an inordinate number of right places at the right times. When Josephine Baker took Paris by storm by appearing almost nude at the Folies Bergère, Anderson was there. In 1928, when W. C. Handy presented a history-making evening of black music (including Fats Waller and James P. Johnson) in Carnegie Hall, Anderson was in the audience. When Red Nichols gave the downbeat to an orchestra full of hot jazz stars in the Gershwins' *Strike Up the Band* on Broadway in 1930, Anderson had an aisle seat. Who got Duke Ellington to present *Black, Brown and Beige* at Carnegie Hall in 1943, then wrote the lyric for "Flamingo"? Anderson, of course. And what family had the beach cabana adjacent to Cole Porter's at the Lido in Venice in the 1920s? None other than the Andersons; Edmund was the son of globe-trotting socialite parents.

So when Anderson, with extraordinary prescience, staged a four-week Cole Porter jamboree some years ago at Manhattan's Citicorp Center, it seemed a sure bet that he would uncover some hitherto forgotten gem or two for the occasion. "Why don't you do 'Let's Step Out?,'" he remarked casually one day to Barbara Lea and Daryl Sherman, one half of the Mister Tram Associates quartet. "No one's done it, at least not lately, and it's a cute song." He was right, of course.

Porter wrote the tune first as "Stepping Out"—very likely the first song he wrote in the decade—and introduced it in *Fifty Million Frenchmen* in March 1930, where it was quickly swamped by "You Do Something to Me," "You've Got That Thing," and "Find Me a Primitive Man." But Anderson—no surprise—was there, and he remembered it.

The ultimate result of all that was this performance, which enlists the vocal talents of two first-rate singers, a tenor saxophonist, and a trumpeter. It is pretty light-hearted stuff, particularly in its more manic moments, but the high spirits and sense of fun are infectious.

Gay Divorce (1932)

After You, Who?
a) Bill Evans
b) Sylvia Syms

"Bill Evans loved Cole Porter," said Helen Keane, who produced the album from which this performance is drawn. "And he loved this tune. He was sorry he hadn't recorded it much earlier. He found it especially interesting because it's so beautifully constructed." Indeed, its rueful, unsentimental flavor seems ideally suited to Evans's lean romanticism.

Those who detect four hands at work here are not hearing things. According to Keane, Evans first set out a basic foundation, outlining harmony and overall melodic shape, then overdubbed a second part, amplifying, embellishing, and commenting on the first. Four hands, one mind: in sum, a remarkable moment.

"It's a very gentle song, a song about necessity," said Sylvia Syms, whose interpretation here is part of an album called *. . . Then Along Came Bill*, dedicated to Evans. "Bill was one of the first pianists I ever heard who seemed almost always related to the lyrics of the songs he was playing. . . . He could capture their essences, in much the way Lester Young did on tenor sax." The spirit and flavor of Evans's work saturate the Syms performance, particularly in Mike Renzi's evocative chording at the outset and understated accompaniment to the vocal.

"After You, Who?" had a special significance for Porter. In casting *Gay Divorce* on Broadway in 1932, he wrote years later to singer George Byron, "Our great hope was to persuade Fred Astaire to play the lead. We were living in Paris at the time and I asked Fred over to the house to hear what I had written so far. Once I had played 'After You,' he decided to do the show." Posterity, even more than Porter himself, was the beneficiary of Astaire's decision.

I've Got You on My Mind
Ambrose and his Orchestra

British music historian Albert McCarthy once remarked in print that he enjoyed Ambrose records of the early 1930s as much as any from the period. In his book, *The Dance Band Era*, he hailed the orchestra's "balance between musical discipline and freedom of individual expression" and added that in 1932 alone, sixty-two Ambrose records were issued, the equivalent of about ten twelve-inch LPs.

Ambrose records—and those by Ray Noble, Lew Stone, and other major British bands of the period—have an unmistakable sound. Recorded in "live" studios, with a greater feeling of spaciousness than their American counterparts, these records evoke a mirrored, shining world of couples clad elegantly in evening clothes, a world in which Fred Astaire and Ginger Rogers (and for that matter Cole Porter) would have been right at home.

Porter apparently wrote "I've Got You on My Mind" as early as 1930 and may have intended to use it first in *The New Yorkers* and then in his unproduced *Star Dust*. But it wound up a highlight of *Gay Divorce*, both the New York and London productions, sung by Astaire and Claire Luce. It is a simple melody, based almost entirely on chord tones. As Alec Wilder described it in *American Popular Song*, "There's nothing unexpected about it. It's simply delightful and it swings."

Sam Browne has a couple of awkward moments at first in negotiating the hill-and-dale melodic line, then settles down comfortably. The eight-bar trumpet solo in the chorus that follows is by the highly regarded Max Goldberg, and there is an engaging glimpse of alto sax by either Danny Polo or Sid Phillips.

Mister and Missus Fitch
Julie Wilson and William Roy

Who *were* Mr. and Mrs. S. Beach Fitch of Tulsa, Oklahoma? Were they real people? Where were all the stories of their mad social climbing coming from? And why on earth hadn't anyone heard of them before? When items about them

Ladies of the chorus in Gay Divorce, *1932.*

Bill Evans in 1958.

started appearing in the Paris edition of the *New York Herald*, readers began to wonder. Here they were, this devil-may-care couple, traveling gaily abroad in the midst of the depression; taking the waters at exclusive spas; giving lavishly to charity; having an audience at the Vatican with Pope Pius XI. Even dining with—yes, indeed—Mr. and Mrs. Cole Porter. What was going on?

Diatribes from the outspoken Mr. Fitch had been appearing with some regularity in the letters columns of various newspapers, usually railing about subjects dear, as he put it, to the heart of every "100 percent American." More than once he tangled with other correspondents, particularly a Mr. Edward Empire, who averred that Mr. Fitch and those like him "are the fundamental cause of all the misunderstandings between nations, unspeakable wars, financial depressions, unemployment, bootlegging, misery and bad art that we have in the world today."

The whole thing was of course a hoax, perpetrated by Cole Porter and various of his friends, notably hostess Elsa Maxwell and Elsie de Wolfe, better known as Lady Mendl. The hoax apparently gave birth to the song, one of Porter's most gleefully wicked. He included it first in his unproduced show *Star Dust*, then recycled it for *Gay Divorce*. Shortly before the show opened, Porter revealed to columnists Walter Winchell and Cholly Knickerbocker that the Fitches were fictitious, thus guaranteeing the song another burst of publicity.

Luella Gear, who sang "Mister and Missus Fitch" in *Gay Divorce*, told Robert Kimball many years later that she paid the pit drummer $5 a week to cover the words "bitch" and "son of a bitch" with a loud, burlesque-style rimshot and cymbal crash, thereby rendering the offending portions all the more tantalizing to audiences.

For all the attention, "Mister and Missus Fitch" never quite caught on and was not published until 1954. Perhaps, in a nation resolutely dedicated to upward mobility, it cut just a bit close to the bone. As Will Rogers remarked at about the same time all this was going on, depression-era America seemed determined to become the only nation in history to go to the poorhouse in an automobile.

Pianist William Roy, best known as one of the premier accompanists in the cabaret business, partners Julie Wilson vocally in this witty retelling of the Fitches' sad story.

Night and Day
Fred Astaire

Cole Porter gave two accounts of how this, one of his most eloquent songs, came to be written. In one, he was inspired to take pen to paper after hearing a muezzin's call to worship from a mosque in Morocco. In the other, rather less colorful version, the melody came to him one Saturday night at the Ritz-Carlton Hotel, and he added a lyric the following day as he lay sunning himself on a beach at Newport.

Fred Astaire introduced it—and danced it with Claire Luce—in *Gay Divorce*, his last appearance on the Broadway stage. Whatever Porter says about the song's origins, said Benny Green in *Let's Face the Music*, "the true points of importance about 'Night and Day' concern, not the monotony of Moroccan religious chanting but the unorthodox deployment of a 48-bar duration in place of the conventional 32; the masterly compression of the vocal range to suit Fred Astaire's vocal style; the witty variations on the theme of night following day in the lyric; the daring perversity of the structure of the song's verse, with its one note repeated 33 times over an 8-bar span, followed by a note a semitone higher played 29 consecutive times."

The song was a sensation from the start. "I am mad about 'Night and Day,' and I think it is your high spot," Irving Berlin wrote in a letter dated 3 January 1933. "You probably know it is being played all over, and all the orchestra leaders think it is the best tune of the year—and I agree with them." So, apparently, did the public; sheet music sales boomed, and records appeared regularly. Even writer Ring Lardner, railing against what he saw as unbridled salaciousness and double entendre in popular song lyrics, won added publicity for "Night and Day" by declaring that the line "There's an oh, such a hungry yearning burning inside of me" was little short of pornographic.

Astaire recorded the song twice within six months. This first effort, backed by Leo Reisman's society orchestra, was No. 1 on the hit parade for ten weeks, before being supplanted by Bing Crosby's recording of "You're Getting to Be a Habit with Me."

He comes across here a bit jauntily for the content of the song, but nevertheless in firm control. What impresses above all is his rhythmic assurance. As Roy Hemming and David Hajdu put it in *Discovering the Great Singers of Classic Pop*, "he phrased naturally and clearly, in a way that was simultaneously relaxed, graceful, elegant, witty, sincere and thoroughly engaging."

Singer Sylvia Syms nailed it perhaps best by commenting that Astaire "danced words. He carried the grace of his dancing over into his singing. No matter what he sang, it always had movement." His phrasing of the words, "Like the beat beat beat of the tom-tom" provides ample illustration of her point.

Night and Day
Billie Holiday

Billie Holiday's singularity as an interpreter of popular songs is in several respects hard to classify. She did not have much by way of vocal attributes. A fellow singer, perhaps

Ethel Waters (documentation is by no means clear), reportedly commented that Billie "sang as if her shoes were too tight." It is beyond argument that she had little range, little suppleness, and occasionally muddled diction. When she said, "I have to change a tune to my way of doing it," she was speaking from a keen instinctive knowledge of her limitations.

In the words of Henry Pleasants, "She had to fit a song not only to herself, but to her state of mind and body, and . . . also to a meager voice—small, hoarse at the bottom and thinly shrill at the top, with top and bottom never very far apart. She had hardly more than an octave and a third."

Perhaps this last also explains why she does as well as she does with "Night and Day," its range determined by Fred Astaire's relatively small vocal compass. As trumpeter-critic Humphrey Lyttelton has put it, Billie's readings of songs were "not so much interpretations as transformations." She makes a song her own by recasting it, inside and out, in her image. When she sings "in the silence of my lonely room," the room pictured in a listener's imagination is a far different room from the one evoked when Astaire sings the line. Holiday's room may be lit by a lone electric light bulb; the wallpaper is faded and peeling. Outside a dusty window there is traffic, or the eternal clatter and screech of the el, or perhaps just an air shaft.

Somehow she makes it live. In her hands, "Night and Day" is as much about Billie and her world as it has been about Astaire and his, and that is the glory of this recording—and the song. The pianist here is Joe Sullivan, working in a subdued manner occasionally reminiscent of Teddy Wilson, with whom Billie made some of her greatest records of the 1930s.

Night and Day
Art Tatum

"Remember," Dick Hyman said in a recent conversation, "Art Tatum was a songs person. His basic repertoire was show tunes and standards. Even though he applied many of the same stylistic features to different songs, he loved to play the songs anyway. To reharmonize them and take them far away from the composers' limitations into new areas." That, of course, is a pianist talking, one whose virtuosity rivals that of Tatum himself. All the same, it reflects one truth basic to songs by Porter and other major writers: the more ingenious, the more original a song, the more it challenges and inspires a gifted jazz improviser to peer beneath its surface.

Tatum seems to have derived particular satisfaction from parsing and reconstructing songs with a technical facility that made him the envy of many a classical pianist. In Gunther Schuller's words, "The note-perfect clarity of Tatum's runs, the hardly believable leaps to the other registers of the piano, . . . his deep-in-the-keys full piano sonority, the tone and touch control in pyrotechnical passages . . . are miracles of performance which must be appreciated aurally."

Such wizardry has drawn its share of criticism over the years, particularly from those who see Tatum's decorative urge as obfuscation. Even Schuller vouchsafed that "Tatum's spectacular right hand only rarely could be restrained to state simple themes or motives. . . . It seemed always in need of exploding into cascading runs and arpeggios, into careening arabesques."

What sets this brief exploration of "Night and Day" apart from other Tatum performances (including his other recordings of the song) is its relative spareness. He sets out the melody over walking left-hand tenths and never quite loses sight of it. As an added delight, it is in the occasionally awkward key of D. Awkward, that is, for pianists other than Tatum. "He'd play in any key that took his fancy," says Hyman. "Even songs he was well known for, he'd play and record several times in different keys. It was all the same to him."

How's Your Romance?
Bobby Short

"I first heard this sung by Lena Horne," Bobby Short said not long ago. "She was using it in her nightclub act around 1956. I thought it very catchy—particularly in the tempo she employed. So I did it at that tempo, too. I still find it a very witty song. Porter's romance with Italy is so apparent here. It's just a delight."

Perhaps unjustly, "How's Your Romance?," sung in *Gay Divorce* with great brio by character actor Erik Rhodes as Tonetti, was buried in all the publicity and general noise surrounding "Night and Day." It also did not help that the show drew mixed notices from the New York papers. The *Post*'s John Mason Brown lamented that not since the failure of *Here Goes the Bride* (music and lyrics by "Body and Soul" writers Johnny Green and Ed Heyman) had "a musical show that seemed promising in advance turn out to be as dull a disappointment as did *Gay Divorce*."

Astaire's performance in the show, said the *Sun*'s Richard Lockridge, gave "a curious impression of unemployment." All the same, *Gay Divorce* turned out to be one of the longest-running musicals of 1932. For the film, it was retitled *The Gay Divorcée*—Hollywood's gray heads were nervous about the idea that anyone should be seen actually to *enjoy* a divorce, but a divorcée having a good time was another matter. The movie was a success, though "How's Your Romance?," along with every other song but "Night and Day," was dropped along the way.

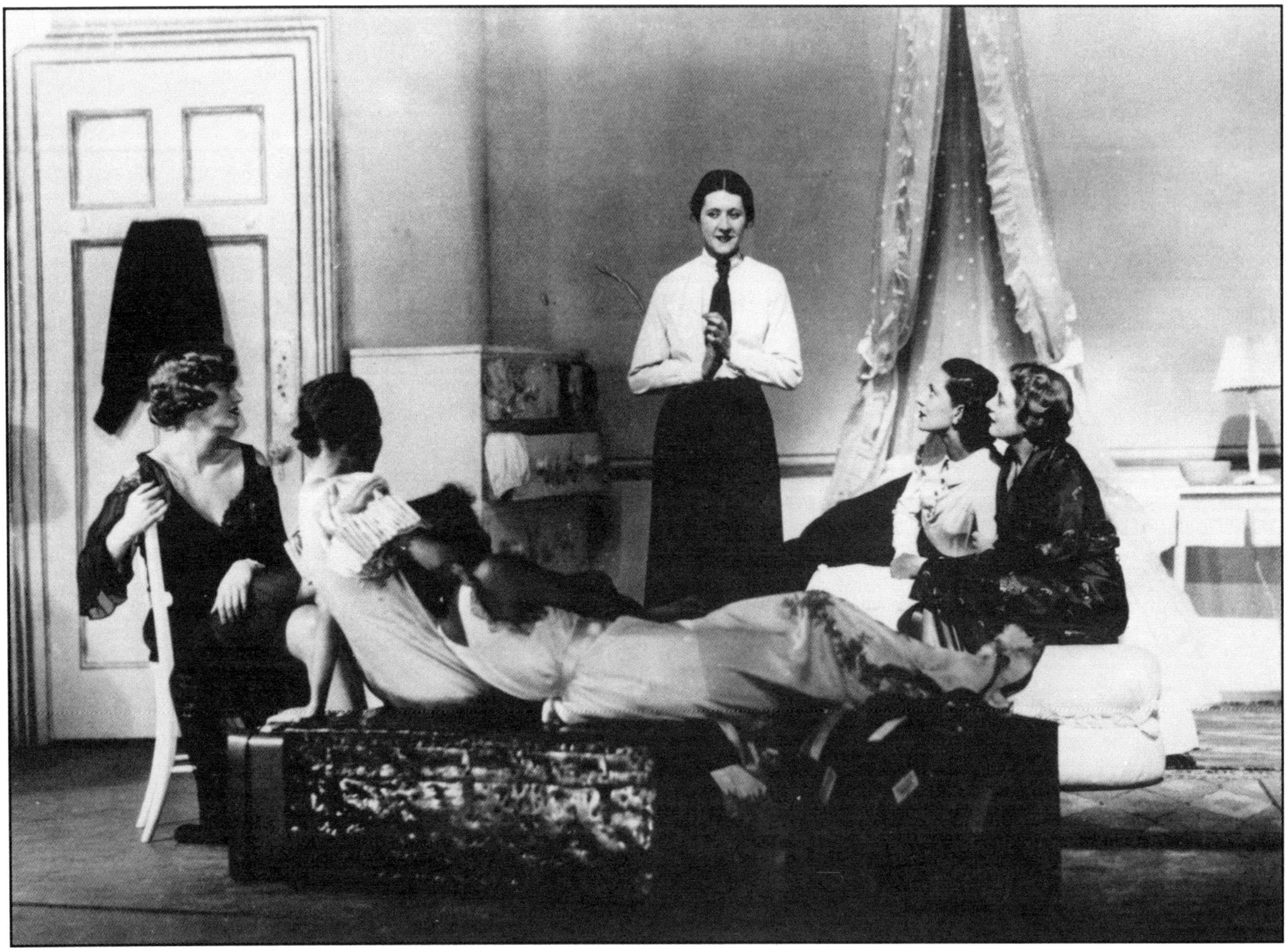

Moya Nugent sings "Experiment" in Nymph Errant. *Gertrude Lawrence is seated to Nugent's left.*

Art Tatum.

Bobby Short has fun here with the Italian phrases of the verse, setting the stage for a performance of infectious high spirits.

Nymph Errant (1933)

Cole Porter rated *Nymph Errant* his favorite among his own shows. It had everything: a scintillating book, following avid but hapless Evangeline as she goes from French impresario to Italian count to Russian fiddler and Turkish businessman in search of a seducer; a sparkling cast, headed by Gertrude Lawrence; Agnes de Mille's choreography; Porter's buoyant and witty music.

Yet *Nymph Errant* never had much of a life beyond the rather modest 154 performances of its London run. Sheridan Morley, biographer of both Lawrence and Noël Coward, suggests that "the utter Englishness of the heroine denied the show an afterlife either on Broadway or on film." But other shows with undeniably English themes—not least *Private Lives* and several others among Coward's best-known works—have done well here, and *Nymph Errant* did not do all that well even in London. It seems more likely that the open and nonjudgmental treatment of female sexuality in *Nymph Errant* simply collided with English and American notions of sexual morality. To adapt a phrase, *Nymph Errant* would never have played in Bournemouth or Peoria.

Experiment
Mabel Mercer

"What is it about Mabel Mercer?," a young singer schooled in today's pop world asked not long ago. "She didn't have much of a voice, did she? And all those mannerisms. And what about her diction—all those stagy rolled 'r's. Yet everybody worships her. What am I missing?"

Well, just about everything. Perhaps the beginning of an explanation of Mabel Mercer lies in the simple observation that she was a thoroughly adult performer, dealing in the thoroughly adult sentiments of thoroughly adult songs.

Not adult in the sense of sexual explicitness or license: that is easy to achieve, particularly these days, and it does not take much maturity. Alec Wilder, that uncompromising observer of music and musicians, expressed it best. Mabel Mercer, he said, "transmutes popular song to the extent that by means of her taste, phrasing and intensity it becomes an integral part of legitimate music. When she sings a song, it is instantly ageless."

The Mercer mystique also has to do with what critic Whitney Balliett has termed her "queenly aura . . . her easy, alabaster technique—the ingenious phrasing, the almost elocutionary diction, the dynamics . . . the graceful melodic push, the quick rhythmic sense, and, as always, the utter authority."

But even all that does not quite explain the magic, the ability to turn a song into an experience immediately relevant to the life of each listener. In some singers' hands, "Experiment" comes across as little more than either an essay in arch double entendre or an exercise in M. Scott Peck–style pop inspiration. Sung by Mabel Mercer it is neither, but instead is a knowing and generous bit of wisdom, based on long experience and offered as a gift to anyone perceptive and adult enough to accept it.

That is not so far afield from the intention of the science mistress, Miss Pratt, who, played by Moya Nugent, sings the song to a young and impressionable Evangeline Edwards, played by Gertrude Lawrence, in *Nymph Errant*. Evangeline hears it as her justification in dashing out into the world in search of defloration, which suited both Porter's needs and those of playwright Romney Brent. But it is a tribute to Mabel Mercer—and to the song—that the lessons of "Experiment" are both longer lasting and more widely applicable than that.

The Cocotte
Cole Porter

Porter's musical lament about the dwindling fortunes of an aging courtesan, and his dry, understated performance, strongly evoke the flavor of W. S. Gilbert (1836–1911), whose wit and facility with light lyrics left their effect on several generations of songwriters. Such lines as "Just a cheated, defeated cocotte am I/On the page of this age, just a blot am I," recall moments from the best of Gilbert's collaborations with Sir Arthur Sullivan (1842–1900) in *Pirates of Penzance*, *HMS Pinafore*, and even *The Mikado*. Benny Green, in fact, cites the moment in *The Sorcerer*, when Wells ("My name is John Wellington Wells/I'm a dealer in magic and spells") sings,

> Then, if you plan it, he
> Changes organity
> With an urbanity
> Full of Satanity,
> Vexes humanity
> With an inanity
> Fatal to vanity,
> Driving your foes to the verge of insanity.

Porter came close to paraphrasing this very lyric years later in "Let's Not Talk about Love," the song that Danny

Kaye introduced in the 1941 musical, *Let's Face It*. Overall, as one critic noted after the London opening of *Nymph Errant*, such songs as "The Cocotte" display "quite a Gilbertian sparkle . . . that delights the ear and is full of the joy of living."

Porter's performance is one of eight he recorded for Victor in late 1934 and early 1935, accompanying himself at the piano. For all its abundant cleverness and popularity in the show, "The Cocotte," which was introduced by Queenie Leonard, has never been published as a separate song.

Nymph Errant
Gertrude Lawrence

Cole Porter and Noël Coward were friends, bound together by mutual respect, by the high life they both enjoyed, by the circles in which they traveled, even by a certain similarity of outlook in the matter of writing songs. Coward was a guest of Porter's in Venice, where Elsa Maxwell, ever quick with a clever nickname, dubbed them "Noëly and Coley."

Each apparently took delight in ribbing the other. Coward's supplementary lyrics to Porter's "Let's Do It, Let's Fall in Love" and "Let's Fly Away" are classics; Porter in *Jubilee* caricatured a fashionable English playwright named Eric Dare, a thinly disguised Coward. As Benny Green puts it, "the two men had much in common, both as versifiers and as personalities, and to a limited degree could be said to be mirror images, Porter representing the chic of America between the wars, and Coward the same qualities of Great Britain in that age. Each possessed complete mastery of the most demanding of all aspects of the songwriting art, the ability to put words to his own melodies, and each took pleasure in casting himself as the detached urbane darling of society commenting waspishly on its foibles."

Porter's admiration for the English polymath even took the form of outright emulation. The title song from *Nymph Errant*, added before the show's London opening, fairly trumpets its debt to Coward, especially in this performance by Gertrude Lawrence, a favorite of both men.

Her essence, so many years after her death, is a bit elusive. The records, though spirited, do not reveal a great singer. A few surviving film clips hint at an engaging insouciance, but little more. Yet "Gertie," as an adoring public loved to call her, was long the toast of the English theatrical world, a much beloved figure even in the United States.

Leave it to Agnes de Mille, whose first assignment as a choreographer involved *Nymph Errant*, to bring Miss Lawrence into the focus of a dancer's eye. "She is funny, bright, touching, irresistible," De Mille wrote. "When she walks, she streams; when she kicks, she flashes. Her speaking voice is a kind of song, quite unrealistic but lovely, and her pathos cuts under all, direct and sudden. Her eyes fill, her throat grows husky, she trembles with wonder. The audience weeps. She can't sing, but who cares?"

The Physician
Joan Morris and William Bolcom

This most endearing of Porter's "list" songs makes inspired mischief out of some unlikely raw material: the vocabulary of a medical textbook, in particular that part of it pertaining to the human anatomy. It delighted audiences and critics at *Nymph Errant*'s London opening, though one reviewer said his general response to the show was "like the physician of whom Miss Lawrence . . . so daringly sings: he loved every detail of her physiological system, but failed to love her as a whole." Whether he simply chose to ignore the rather salacious pun lodged within that phrase in the lyric is lost to history.

All the same, "The Physician" was a hit. A gossip columnist of the time, stoking the fires, informed the public with a straight face that Gertrude Lawrence "found it advisable to have a doctor present . . . at her theatrical rehearsals, in case she wanted to refresh her memory about the pronunciation of such medical terms as epiglottis, vermiformis, lymphatics, epidermis and esophagus."

Porter wrote "The Physician" under the title "But He Never Says He Loves Me" in 1930 for *The New Yorkers*, but the song did not survive the pre-Broadway tryouts. He had intended to use it in *Star Dust* the following year, but put it back in the trunk after the show lost its backing and was abandoned.

Joan Morris, here accompanied by her husband William Bolcom, brings just the right amount of coquettishness to this performance, managing to convey innocence and wicked intent in more or less equal measure.

How Could We Be Wrong?
Bobby Short

"No one," Bobby Short said recently, "could write a love song like Porter. He really knew how to lay it on the line. Total adoration." It seems incongruous at first that the smart sophisticate of "The Physician" and "The Cocotte" could also, in the same show, deliver a love song that works so effectively on so many emotional levels as "How Could We Be Wrong?"

It manages to project, at once, a kind of innocence *and* a doggedly eager hope that after any number of failures and broken hearts, this romance has to be the one that works. It is both idealistic and very knowing. "It's totally innocent, very

Bobby Short.

bare," said Short. "It can clutch at your heart. Listening to it, reading the lyric, you find yourself wanting the affair to work, determined that it will, somehow."

There is no doubt that under all the wit and brittle worldliness lived an innocent and rather ardently true blue Cole Porter. "A lot of people thought that Cole was a strange man—cold, indifferent, rude," wrote Ada Smith in her autobiography, *Bricktop*, the name by which she was known to the society and entertainment world of the 1930s. "He was shy, and shy people have problems, especially if they're prominent. . . . I don't care to speculate about what made Cole Porter tick. I only know he was a good friend to me, one of the best friends I've ever had."

Elisabeth Welch, who stopped the show in *Nymph Errant* with the riotous "Solomon," agreed: "He was a dear, sweet man, and terribly shy; you wanted to get it perfect for him, because you saw he was so sensitive."

Short's reading of the lyric of "How Could We Be Wrong?" abounds with small, totally appropriate touches. The way he delivers the lines in the verse: "Could this be my long-lost dream come true?/The moment we touched, I knew," is saturated with yearning. And when at the very end he moves to his upper register, as ultimately he must, the emotional urgency is compelling indeed.

Solomon
Elisabeth Welch

Elisabeth Welch had already tasted stardom when Cole Porter summoned her to England to sing his harem song, "Solomon," in *Nymph Errant*. She had introduced "Charleston" ("The song, honey, not the dance") in *Runnin' Wild* (1923) on Broadway, worked in Lew Leslie's *Blackbirds of 1928* alongside Adelaide Hall and Bill "Bojangles" Robinson, and stepped into *The New Yorkers* to stop the show (and, it turned out, the censors) with "Love for Sale."

As she understood it, she told an interviewer in 1986, one of Porter's diplomat friends took him to coffee in a harem belonging to a sultan in some unnamed Middle Eastern country. "And he heard this noise in the background—'ah, aaaaah, ah aaaaah,' and he kept it in his head. When he got out, he wrote it down, tucked it in a little pigeonhole. He came to see me, you know, 'the girl who took over,' and said he had an idea for me."

"One-song Welch," her own nickname for herself, did "Solomon" and created a sensation. The *Guardian* praised her "gusto, highly infectious." Another critic, writing in the *Chronicle*, opined, "If Elisabeth Welch had had half a dozen songs to sing she would have stolen the show."

She was still singing "Solomon," along with "Love for Sale" and the rest when, during the 1980s, she dazzled New York audiences in *Black Broadway* and in her own one-woman show. Perhaps Bobby Short, a lifelong admirer, summed her up best in lauding "the understated elegance and simplicity that have marked everything she's ever done. After all, isn't simplicity a major part of true elegance?"

It's Bad for Me
Rosemary Clooney and the Benny Goodman Sextet

It is safe to say that Benny Goodman's efforts as a vocalist will never seriously challenge his immortality as a clarinetist and bandleader. But the King of Swing, in common with such other jazz instrumentalists as Jack Teagarden, Bunny Berigan, and—the master of them all—Louis Armstrong, sang quite engagingly. Like them, he made up in impeccable phrasing what he might have lacked in vocal quality.

Goodman's first known vocal on record is a 1930 effort on a forgettable pop tune called "Linda," though he told at least one interviewer that during his four years as a sideman with Ben Pollack in the 1920s he often sang on radio broadcasts. Benny's vocals on such records as "Gotta Be This or That" and "All the Cats Join In" by his own band are charming and well known.

Goodman's interest in recording "It's Bad for Me" dates back to a 1955 recording session for his own short-lived Park Recording Company. They had run the tune down with vocalist Nancy Reed, and apparently things were not going as Goodman had hoped. Trumpeter Ruby Braff recalled suggesting to Goodman that he take over some of the vocal, turning it into a duet. "He was kind of reluctant," said Braff, "but he tried it, and it sounded fine."

That recording was never issued, but Goodman liked "It's Bad for Me" sufficiently to sell Columbia on the idea of recording it. Rosemary Clooney was Columbia's hot vocalist of the moment, riding high with "Come on-a My House" and other hits, so she landed the date.

"We rehearsed in the apartment on 57th Street that Rosie had with her husband at the time, José Ferrer," said Dick Hyman, pianist and arranger on the date. "I only knew Benny as a singer through the little bit he used to do with Martha Tilton on 'Loch Lomond,' which wasn't much. Yet here he was singing a duet with Rosie Clooney, and doing just great. It knocked me out."

This performance was a history-making record for a couple of additional reasons not strictly connected with music. The four titles made that day were the last to be issued by Columbia on 78 rpm; with the addition of two further selections, they also became part of the last original-issue ten-inch Goodman LP released in the United States.

It is a relaxed, flowing performance. Benny sets out the melody on clarinet, with trumpeter Buck Clayton taking the bridge. A quick modulation brings on the vocal, with Benny

Gertrude Lawrence (on divan) and Elisabeth Welch, who introduced "Solomon" in Nymph Errant.

Elisabeth Welch in 1931.

Ethel Merman in 1934, when she starred in Anything Goes.

Porter's 1931 typescript for "I Get a Kick Out of You," with corrections made after the Lindbergh kidnapping in 1932.

"I GET A KICK OUT OF YOU"

Verse:—

My story is much too sad to tell
But practically everything leaves me totally cold
The only exception I know is the nights
That I'm out on a quiet spree
Fighting vainly the old ennui
And I suddenly return and see your fabulous face.

Refrain:—

I get no kick from champagne
Mere alcohol doesn't thrill me at all
So tell me why should it be true
That I get a kick out of you
Some get a kick from cocaine
I'm sure that if I took even one sniff
That would bore me terrific'ly too,
Yet I get a kick out of you.
I get a kick every time I see you
Standing there before me,
I get a kick though it's clear to me
You obviously don't adore me
I get no kick in a plane
~~I shouldn't care for those nights in the air~~
~~That the fair Mrs. Lindbergh goes through~~
But I get a kick out of you.

→ Flying too high with some
   guy in the sky
Is my idea of nothing t[o]

and Rosie trading phrases; Urbie Green solos on trombone for half a chorus, and the two vocalists return for a rousing finale.

Anything Goes (1934)

Anything Goes
Cole Porter

The musical that became *Anything Goes* sprang from a simple but appealing recipe: take an ocean liner loaded with zany characters, add a bomb threat and lots of comic high jinks, mix well, and let simmer. With a book by P. G. Wodehouse and Guy Bolton, various antics by the comedy team of William Gaxton and Victor Moore, Ethel Merman as star, and Cole Porter as lyricist-composer, how could it miss?

It was a particularly timely notion. The French Line had launched its new eighty-thousand-ton *Normandie* in late 1932, heralding what appeared to be a new age in transatlantic luxury ship travel. Combining, in one writer's words, "the splendor of Versailles with the grace of a yacht," the *Normandie* seemed to laugh at the depression, to proclaim that some things—even if outside the reach of the common man—were eternal. Cunard's introduction of its stately *Queen Mary* a year later simply underscored the point.

So why not, particularly for Americans sick of austerity and deprivation, stage an elaborate Broadway musical that emphasized the fun, the luxury, and some of the danger in life on board an ocean liner?

It seemed a great idea, until disaster struck. On 8 September 1934 the luxury ship *Morro Castle* caught fire and burned off Asbury Park, New Jersey, with a loss of 130 lives. All at once a Broadway musical threatening a shipwreck seemed a rather less salutary notion.

Producer Vinton Freedley was desperate; too much money had been invested to turn back, so the show's book would have to be drastically rewritten. With Bolton and Wodehouse out of the country, he turned to his director Howard Lindsay, himself a playwright with a couple of respectable successes to his name. Lindsay agreed to take on the task, on condition that Freedley find him a collaborator to share the load. Such a person duly turned up in Russel "Buck" Crouse, the Theater Guild's press agent. Crouse had helped create *Hold Your Horses*, a hit the previous year for Broadway comic Joe Cook.

So the musical that had started life as *Hard to Get*, been known briefly as *Bon Voyage*, and survived the *Morro Castle* disaster opened at last in Boston on 5 November 1934 with the two writers scribbling revisions right up to curtain time.

As for the final name of both show and song, Crouse says it was born when William Gaxton was asked whether he would mind making his entrance a moment after opening curtain. "In this kind of spot," said Gaxton, "anything goes."

Cole Porter recalled it somewhat differently. He told biographer Richard Hubler that "Gaxton, coming through the stage door one night, plaintively demanded of the doorkeeper, 'What are we going to call this musical mishmash?' The doorkeeper shrugged, grinned, and said, 'Well, you know, Mr. Gaxton, anything goes.'"

Whatever the case, as the circumstances attending the birth of the show indicated, times were changing, and who was better able to chronicle that, with unfailing attention to detail, than Porter? "Anything Goes" is a deft and engaging rhythm song with a telling and rather wicked lyric. Porter delivers it here with affection and obvious relish.

I Get a Kick Out of You
Ethel Merman

"As a singer," Ethel Merman wrote in her first autobiography, *Who Could Ask for Anything More?*, "I do one basic thing. I project. That means that I belt the lyrics over the footlights like a baseball coach belting flyballs to an outfield. . . . I don't bother about style, but I do bother about making people understand the lyrics I sing. I honestly don't think there's anyone in the business who can top me at that."

Probably not—at least not when it came to putting across a song as its composer intended it to be heard. No surprise, then, that Porter, Irving Berlin, and Ira Gershwin waxed rhapsodic about her. "She has the finest enunciation of any American singer I know," Porter told the *New York Times* in 1936. Merman reciprocated by telling the world, "I'd rather sing his songs than those by any other writer."

The enunciation that so beguiled Porter comes in handy in "I Get a Kick Out of You," her great opener in *Anything Goes*. How else to deal with a mouthful like "terrifically"? Her solution is easy: pause briefly after the second syllable, effectively cutting the word in half. "It was just a way of phrasing," she wrote, "of breaking a word into syllables and holding one syllable longer than I ordinarily would, but for some reason that pause killed the people. I'm not enough of a musician to know why, but I know it had that effect."

Henry Pleasants, in *The Great American Popular Singers*, offers an answer. "Miss Merman, here, has just given an instructive example of *tempo rubato*, the stealing of time," he wrote. "What she did was steal time from *icly* [ically] and give it to *rif*, achieving not only emphasis, but also surprise and suspense. The listener instinctively perceived the theft, and was impatient to see how the loss would be made good."

William Gaxton and Ethel Merman sing "You're the Top" in Anything Goes.

The Hal Kemp Orchestra in the early 1930s.

"I Get a Kick Out of You" had been around since 1931. Like "The Physician," "Mister and Missus Fitch," and "I've Got You on My Mind," it had been part of Porter's unproduced *Star Dust* and was saved for later use. Porter's original lyric included the line, "I get no kick in a plane./I shouldn't care for those nights in the air/That the fair Mrs. Lindbergh goes through." After the kidnapping and subsequent murder of the Lindbergh baby in 1932, the Lone Eagle and his family were no longer considered fair game for such frivolities, and the lyric was changed.

Similarly, "Some get a kick from cocaine" ran afoul of the censors and had to be removed for radio play, a restriction that remained in place for many years. Among Porter's substitutes were "whiff of Guerlain," "perfumes of Spain," and later even "bop-type refrain," though one wonders if he ever spent an evening listening to Charlie Parker or Dizzy Gillespie.

All through the Night
Barbara Lea with Bucky Pizzarelli

Leave it to Alec Wilder, in *American Popular Song*, to point out that in the 64 bars (double the standard length) that make up this surprisingly complex song, there are only eight intervals that are not chromatic. As Wilder reads it, that shows Porter's craft: "The fact that these half-step melodic lines manage to maintain tension throughout and not fall away into affectedness indicates the mastery of the writing . . . it's as if Porter were rising to his feet in a crowded room and calling out, 'Here I am!'" Had Porter done things even slightly differently, he adds, "All through the Night" could have been "an arty piece of melodrama. But it isn't."

For Barbara Lea, the chromatic, compressed nature of the melodic line gives the song its almost hypnotic quality. "Take the verse," she said recently. "The 'monotone of the evening's drone.' . . . Like the verse of 'Night and Day,' which it resembles, this one actually expresses what the song is about. . . . Also Porter was particularly good at expressing the idea of being with someone only in dreams. Look at 'Dream Dancing,' and even 'Night and Day.' The dream world takes on a life of its own."

Barbara Lea and guitarist Bucky Pizzarelli recorded "All through the Night" at the end of a session at which she was accompanied by a seven-piece jazz band. "It was late. All the guys had gone home except Bucky and me," she said. "I was sitting, not standing, singing with my eyes closed in a kind of trancelike state. The song, and what we were doing with it, was a living thing. It was spellbinding. That's what the song is about, really: 'But then once again I can dream I've the right/To be close to you all through the night.' Utterly magical."

Blow, Gabriel, Blow
Ethel Merman

Sometime toward the end of the 1920s, Tin Pan Alley discovered southern revival meetings. All at once, pop songs were loaded with exhortations like Sam Coslow and W. Franke Harling's "Sing You Sinners." Jazz trumpeter Red Nichols recorded a two-sided version of Andy Razaf's "On Revival Day," featuring Jack Teagarden as a deacon proclaiming that "When that congregation starts to sing/Nothin' in this world don't mean a thing." The sense of exultation, of uninhibited joy that saturated even the idea of a revival meeting held limitless appeal for an urban white public still shedding its Victorian roots.

All the same that the image was in great part a press agent's fancy, that real-life revival and camp meetings were as much a phenomenon of the white South as of the black. Hand-clapping songs proclaiming redemption and purifyin' heavenly angels continued to pour off the music publishers' presses.

Truth or fiction, the idea fascinated Cole Porter, that city dweller *par excellence*, and he made two attempts to express his fascination in song. One came in 1950 in "Climb up the Mountain" ("and lay your burden down") from *Out of This World*. The other, and most successful effort was this blockbuster from *Anything Goes*, sung—or, perhaps more appropriately, trumpeted—by the irrepressible Ethel Merman. Love her or loathe her, she is a commanding presence: it is hard to imagine anyone else better suited to Porter's brand of sermonizing. As Roy Hemming and David Hajdu put it in *Discovering Great Singers of Classic Pop*, "Big and brassy and full of pizzazz, she was the very image of the street-smart New York dame who epitomized Broadway in the early '30s."

Merman made this recording in 1947 (starring, at the time, in *Annie Get Your Gun*), thirteen years after the Broadway success of *Anything Goes*. By then she was, if anything, louder and brassier—but also far more confident—than she had been in 1934. The song is clearly hers: attempts by others (band vocalist George "Bon Bon" Tunnell and English jazz trumpeter Nat Gonella among them) suffered by comparison. They, and several dance band leaders as well, found the song did not travel well outside the context of the show.

The Porter-Merman relationship became a lifelong friendship as well as a fruitful professional collaboration. "I had no idea, really, at the time how much he meant to me, [not only] as a writer of great songs but as a friend," she told Robert Kimball in the early 1970s. "I miss him now more than ever."

You're the Top
Hal Kemp and his Orchestra

A writer in *The New Yorker* was quick to spot the potential in this most famous of Porter's "list songs" around the time *Anything Goes* opened. "Mr. Porter is in a class by himself as a writer of original lyrics," he said, "and unless I do not know my theatregoers, the town will shortly be driving itself crazy trying to memorize the series of things indicating the 'Top.' In this one song, [Porter] has summarized American civilization better than any symposium of national thinkers has ever been able to do."

Indeed, "You're the Top" quickly graduated from mere hit to national craze. According to one estimate, would-be wordsmiths were cranking out parodies at the rate of three hundred a month. They turned up in newspapers, in the routines of comedians and, by the bushel, in the composer's mailbox.

On one occasion, it is said, Porter himself devised some extra lyrics for a radio broadcast, only to be turned down. Sorry, said a network official, but because of the large numbers of unauthorized parodies, the composer has forbidden any departures from the original. But I am the composer, Porter protested. Sorry, came the reply—no exceptions, not even for Mr. Cole Porter.

Heard now, the lyric to "You're the Top" evokes feelings akin to those experienced on a leisurely stroll through a shop specializing in "nostalgia" and period bric-a-brac. Arrow collar and Coolidge dollar (who, today, has ever seen one?), National Gallery and Garbo's salary, *Inferno*'s Dante and Great Durante, Waldorf Salad and Berlin ballad, Bendel Bonnet and Shakespeare sonnet—an inventory of an era's ideals of what was classy and distinctive, expressed with ingenuity and decided affection. And, in the case of this Hal Kemp performance, rendered with humor and a fitting sense of style. John Scott Trotter's arrangement calls on the saxophones for some bravura turns, led by the note-perfect alto of Harold "Porky" Dankers, and punctuated by plunger-muted growls from the brass.

Many years later in some record liner notes, writer and record producer Dave Dexter, Jr., would remember his nights standing in front of the Kemp band, marveling at Dankers's "acrobatic leading of the sax and clarinet sections, strictly impossible feats which gained the great admiration of numerous big-name jazz musicians as well as that of dancers and theater patrons."

Kemp's was the third recording of "You're the Top"—both Porter and Paul Whiteman recorded it independently on 26 October 1934. Kemp in fact recorded it twice, once commercially for Brunswick on 6 November 1934 and again, almost identically, for the World Transcription Company a little more than a month later. This transcription version, intended only for radio use, was recorded in a particularly "live" studio, lending the band a broad, expansive sound.

Sometime-drummer Skinnay Ennis sets out the lyrics with clarity and the rather breathless sound that was his trademark. "That was all the voice he had," noted Trotter, later known as longtime musical director for Bing Crosby. "It was just the way he felt a song. I don't think anybody ever sang a song with more or better enunciation than Skinnay did with as little voice as he really had."

You're the Top
Louis Armstrong

What accounts for the marvel of Louis Armstrong? His solo trumpet style established the vocabulary of jazz improvisation for generations to come. Yet it appeared at a time when there were no precedents, no comfortable role models. Armstrong's style was wholly original, tacked together out of what was available to him—whether it was the bravura of a concert-band cornet, or the soaring majesty of an operatic aria heard in an alley behind the opera house in his native New Orleans.

His approach to singing, no less remarkable, was what Henry Pleasants has called "unique and improbable." It has also been uniquely and improbably influential, perhaps even more so than his trumpet playing. Instrumental virtuosity is an abstraction. The notes, phrases, and inflections of a jazzman's art are their own language; in coming to them, an even casual listener must learn at some level to interpret their phrases, cadences, and their relation to the melody and chord sequence.

Singing is different. Popular singing is, after all, words and sentences, thoughts and feelings, all on a far more immediate, hence accessible, level, with no language barrier and no conventions to understand. There is no mystique for the lay listener to penetrate.

It is not improbable to suggest, therefore, that Louis Armstrong's ultimate expressive vehicle was his voice; that even the trumpet, in all its splendor, was an extension of his simple urge to sing. Instead of singing the way he played, Armstrong played the way he sang.

Such a notion readily accounts for his way of instinctively tailoring a melodic line and even a song's text to suit his needs—all somehow without doing them violence. None of this had much to do with conventional, "legitimate" singing; from the standpoint of the voice coach or opera buff, Louis sang quite gloriously "wrong," and as the years passed he got wronger still. The velour textures of what had been, in his twenties, a high baritone, gradually thickened and coarsened, producing a sound identified most often as hoarse, or gravelly.

But no matter. There was never a moment when he did not know how to reach a listener, vocally or instrumentally. On this performance, for example, he opens by proclaiming, "You the Tops!" Yet this alteration and all that follow—in words, syntax, pronunciation, emphasis—function less as distortion than as simple adaptation.

"This is in no way his kind of song," said clarinetist Joe Muranyi in a recent conversation. Muranyi is an Armstrong scholar who worked alongside Louis in the Armstrong All-Stars for the last five years of the great jazzman's life. "God knows why they gave it to him. It's a mouthful of words, most of them having very little to do with any world Louis lived in. He and Cole Porter were miles apart that way—except, maybe, in something like *High Society*.

"But Louis makes it his own anyway. He has great fun with it—without sounding too highfalutin', you could almost say he takes this very fancy song out of the country club and gives it to the common man. A kind of gift."

Armstrong plays no trumpet here. The record is all vocal and high spirits, Louis strolling freely through Porter's sitting room, rearranging furniture, ornament, and decor as suits his whim.

"The thing about Louis, above all, is a most extraordinary generosity of spirit," says Barbara Lea. "There's nothing but love, and joy, and utter pleasure. When he sings, 'You're the Top,' I think he's saying it to each listener, individually. 'I think you're okay,' he seems to be saying, 'so let's all have a fine old time with this song.'"

Miscellaneous Song (1934)

Miss Otis Regrets
Ethel Waters

Songs forever seemed to be occurring to Cole Porter at dinner, at parties, or other even more colorful social occasions. According to one story, he dreamed up the list of superlatives that became "You're the Top" while dining in Paris at Le Boeuf sur Le Toit; another, quoted earlier, had him devising "I Happen to Like New York" aboard an ocean liner.

With that in mind, imagine a convivial gathering at the New York apartment of Porter's Yale classmate, Leonard Hanna. The radio is playing some cowboy lament. Cole, ever impish, parks himself at the piano and starts yodeling a parody, broad and rather wicked. His friend Monty Woolley, always good for a laugh, joins in; the two begin pitching phrases at each other, and at some point it all starts to sound like a song.

Woolley, later to leave his permanent mark on Broadway as Sheridan Whiteside in *The Man Who Came to Dinner*, whoops with boyish mischief as he lifts a morning coat from Hanna's butler and a silver tray from a maid. With Porter's prompting, he begins to sing their handiwork, a tearful tale about poor Miss Otis, an obviously well-bred lady who will have to miss her regular luncheon because of an unavoidable date with the gallows.

Or words to that effect. Elsa Maxwell, touting "Miss Otis Regrets" as a kind of upscale Frankie-and-Johnny song, insisted on having it played and sung at parties in her sprawling, rent-free suite at the Waldorf-Astoria. Perhaps in appreciation, Porter dedicated it to her. The song was a sensation in New York and an instant success abroad, where it turned up in the 1934 English musical *Hi Diddle Diddle* and was even recorded in French by balladeer Jean Sablon.

Ethel Waters's interpretation here represents the only Cole Porter song she ever recorded. Waters had built much of her career in the 1920s and early 1930s on records made for Columbia, including "Dinah," "Birmingham Bertha," "Memories of You," and the fabulously successful "Am I Blue?" Without exception, they were gems—beautifully recorded, with excellent instrumental backings, and issued on high-quality laminated pressings with surfaces so quiet that the music emerged with a clarity that still astonishes the ears.

But in 1932 American Columbia went bankrupt, and after a period of economic and artistic rudderlessness was absorbed by the large and profitable American Record Company. ARC was quite another operation, notorious—even by depression standards—for saving a buck. Its hallmarks included cramped, dead studios, substandard recorded sound, and cheap, noisy pressings on its Brunswick, Melotone, and inappropriately named Perfect labels.

In 1934 Brunswick recording chief Jack Kapp decided to launch his own label, Decca, taking with him a stableful of Brunswick performers. Decca began life with Bing Crosby singing "I Love You Truly" and an artist roster that also included the Dorseys, Guy Lombardo, the Mills Brothers, the Boswell Sisters, the Casa Loma Orchestra, and Ethel Waters.

Miss Waters recorded two dates of four sides each, including a remake of her hit "Dinah," and then was dropped. Why? Given her strong temperament and short fuse (and

Ethel Waters in 1935.

perhaps inflated notion of her own market value), it is not hard to imagine some *contretemps* with Kapp over money, "artistic control," or the like. Her performance here nicely straddles the fence between the worlds of jazz and blues on one side, and the rather more formal conventions of musical theater on the other. She delivers the mock-serious lyric with just a touch of tongue-in-cheek, a healthy irreverence that keeps things from veering off into either melodrama or caricature; she both tells the story and comments on it.

Jazz lovers used to the more natural enunciation and articulation of such black singers as Bessie Smith and Billie Holiday often find the Waters diction mannered, even affected; some have criticized it as a concession to white taste for the sake of success in white show business. But the exaggerated vowels and rolled 'r's must be heard first and foremost as a response to the demands of the theater. Ethel Waters sought the stage and adopted its conventions, much as Elisabeth Welch, Adelaide Hall, and other black theatrical artists of the day did. In the 1930s, with stage miking still far in the future, a singer had to know how to pitch to every seat in the house. White or black, it was all the same: If the customers in the back row could not hear you, you were dead.

Miss Otis Regrets
Ella Fitzgerald

"She has a lovely voice," Henry Pleasants has written of Ella Fitzgerald, "one of the warmest and most radiant in its natural range that I have heard in a lifetime of listening to singers in every category." He goes on, as have countless writers, to laud her intonation, her harmonic sense, her impeccable swing, her inventiveness.

It is a familiar litany, and one that has helped secure Ella's place as the most widely known and loved of all female popular singers. Even her fellow artists have lauded her mastery of every phase of the vocal art. Bing Crosby's pronouncement is typical: "Man, woman and child, Ella Fitzgerald is the greatest." "I never knew how good our songs were," Ira Gershwin has been quoted as saying, "until I heard Ella Fitzgerald sing them." Indeed, Ella brings a sense of rightness, of inevitability, to everything she does.

But for all the praise, there are many Fitzgerald performances in which content, the emotional inner life of a song, seems to take a back seat. It is almost as though her very vocal excellence has kept her from being a great musical actress, or interpreter of lyrics. Leave the introspection to such diverse artists as Billie Holiday, Ethel Waters, Judy Garland, or Sylvia Syms, all of them less generously endowed vocally.

Some writers have compared Ella's apparent emotional detachment to that of her sometime collaborator on records, Louis Armstrong. "Like Louis, she has always seemed to be having a ball," Pleasants has written. "It has been a joyous, exhilarating, memorable, but hardly an emotional experience."

This very aloofness could be said to lend Ella's reading of "Miss Otis" its poignancy. Unlike Ethel Waters, she does not interpret, comment, or otherwise interpose herself between song and listener. Her approach is simple, even innocent— she tells the story and accepts it on its terms. Even the rather girlish quality of her voice seems to lend truth to the fable of love, betrayal, and revenge.

Adios, Argentina (1934–35, unproduced film)

Don't Fence Me In
Edward Nell and the Foursome Quartet

It was Lou Brock, the man who first teamed Fred Astaire with Ginger Rogers in the movies, who approached Porter to write music for a projected cowboy musical called *Adios, Argentina*. Porter went to work on a score, recording six of the songs on demonstration discs at New York's Brunswick studio with baritone Edward Nell and the Foursome vocal quartet from *Anything Goes*.

One of the songs had a particularly interesting conception. The phrase, "Don't Fence Me In," had caught Brock's fancy, and he asked his pal Robert Fletcher, an amateur poet and songwriter who worked for the state of Montana traffic department, to play around with it. If something resulted he should send it to Porter, whom he described as "one of our very best composers, who is rated as high as anyone on Broadway at the present time."

Fletcher, obviously flattered, whipped up a song and sent it off. Porter apparently liked it and, in Brock's words, borrowed its "title and some characteristic words and phrases" in fashioning his own song. Fletcher signed over his rights for $250; Porter, in return, promised Fletcher some form of credit when the song was published.

Fate decreed otherwise. Fox Studios scrubbed *Adios, Argentina*, and "Don't Fence Me In" went on the shelf, to be rediscovered in 1943 by Herman Starr of Warner Bros. Music and sung by Roy Rogers in the World War II morale-building film, *Hollywood Canteen* (1944). Bing Crosby and the Andrews Sisters recorded it for Decca, and the innocuous little ditty became a major hit.

Unhappily, Fletcher's name was left off the published copy, an oversight Porter sought to correct by assigning him a portion of the royalties. Porter introduces this first version of "Don't Fence Me In" with a reference to Lou Brock; this recording is a composite, drawn from two takes so as to feature both Nell and the Foursome.

Don't Fence Me In
Bing Crosby and the Andrews Sisters

The continuing popularity of "Don't Fence Me In" amazed Porter. For him, in conversations with friends, it was just "that old thing." But its homage to simple, basic American values, coming while United States servicemen were fighting in two theaters of war in far-flung corners of the globe, seemed to strike a responsive chord in the American people.

The Crosby–Andrews Sisters record sold in the millions, reaching *Billboard*'s No. 1 slot on 16 December 1944 and remaining there for eight weeks. That success in turn generated similarly handsome sheet-music sales. Was there a GI, whether city or country bred, who did not know it? Indeed, few Porter songs were as universally known and loved.

"Don't Fence Me In" continued to make headlines even as the war began winding down. A 22 January 1945 story in *Newsweek* implied that Bob Fletcher's contribution to the extraordinarily popular song had been minimal. According to another alleged exposé, Fletcher was nothing but an "antediluvian cowboy" trying to cash in on Porter's wealth, success, and reputation. Others, partial to Fletcher, retorted with statements alleging that he was the real composer after all, and that Porter had stolen it and claimed credit.

For a while there seemed no end to the claims and counterclaims. Doubt persisted about the true authorship of "Don't Fence Me In" until 1983, when Robert Kimball published Fletcher's original text in *The Complete Lyrics of Cole Porter*. As Brock had said, Porter had used the "title and some characteristic words and phrases" from Fletcher's text, but that was all.

JUBILEE (1935)

Begin the Beguine
Tony Martin

Despite the enthusiasm of the critics, "Begin the Beguine" was not an overnight hit; its success came gradually, over a matter of years. One reason may have to do with its 108-bar length, unconscionable in a popular-music world used to tying things up in neat little 32- and 64-bar bundles. As Charles Schwartz put it in his Porter biography, "Simply remembering the complete tune became a major hassle for the public . . . even now most people can not sing 'Begin the Beguine' . . . from beginning to end without messing up somewhere along the line."

Not only is just getting through the song a feat (one full chorus usually takes more than three minutes, the standard length for a 78 rpm record), but there are many shifts of mood and emotional texture to negotiate. In fact, "Begin the Beguine" is less a song than a miniature musical psychodrama, moving from simple nostalgia—the dream of a memorable and long-ago *amour*—into a shadowland of regret, yearning, self-castigation, remembered exultation, and, above all, mutability, even mortality. There are moments at which it achieves eloquence: where else in any popular song does a listener find such utterances as "To live it again is past all endeavor"?

Poignant and often subtle touches abound. The singer first pleads, "So don't let them begin the beguine," but rather let the past lie dead. But a moment later he implores, "let them begin the beguine, make them play," in order that "what moments divine, what rapture serene" *not* be allowed to die.

A singer can approach such complexities in one of two ways: either *act* the song, highlighting and underscoring, clarifying its emotional complexities; or, as Tony Martin does here, simply sing the text, allowing the emotional currents to course through the listener's mind without any interpretive interference.

The 108 bars can also be a test of endurance, with climaxes frequent enough to deny a performer any respite. Even such masters as Bing Crosby, Mildred Bailey, and Frank Sinatra have had to pace themselves carefully or make certain compromises in merely staying the course. Martin rises splendidly to the challenge, delivering a strong, ardent, and vocally consistent reading.

Begin the Beguine
Xavier Cugat and his Waldorf-Astoria Orchestra

What fun it would be, Moss Hart found himself thinking one January night in 1935, to write a musical with Cole Porter. He considered a theme, a few ideas—and quickly dismissed the whole notion. What the author of *Face the Music*, *As Thousands Cheer*, and other Broadway hits really needed was not yet another new project, but some time off. Maybe even take a year, go on a 'round-the-world cruise. Wouldn't *that* be something!

He mentioned the idea to Porter. "He looked at me soberly," Hart later recalled. "'Why not do both?' he said. 'I like that idea of yours for a musical. Why don't we do it and go around the world at the same time?'"

So it came to pass that scarcely a week later, Cole Porter boarded the Cunard White Star liner *Franconia* with his wife Linda, Hart, and friends Monty Woolley, William Powell, and Howard Sturges, plus twenty-seven pieces of luggage, a small piano-organ, a typewriter, metronome, phonograph, pencils and manuscript paper, and six cases of Perrier-Jouet champagne. Destination: 'round the world, via the equatorial route.

Bing Crosby and the Andrews Sisters.

Porter with the Foursome Quartet early in 1935, during recording sessions for Adios, Argentina.

Xavier Cugat with his orchestra at the Waldorf-Astoria Hotel in the 1930s.

June Knight sings "Begin the Beguine" in Jubilee.

The cruise produced *Jubilee* and a score with some of Porter's most lasting and beloved hits. "Begin the Beguine," he said, came to him after he witnessed a native dance at the village of Kalabahi, on the island of Alor in the Dutch East Indies. Hart more or less corroborated this by recalling Porter, seated at the piano-organ in his cabin, playing and singing the new song as the *Franconia* steamed toward the Fiji Islands.

Porter later added to the story, saying his first inspiration had been a mid-1920s visit to an out-of-the-way Paris nightclub to see the blacks of Martinique dance something called the "beguine." He wrote that the "beguine" was derived from a Martinique native dance called the "bel-air." It was performed at balls where the leader would set the rhythm with a drum and then start the dance with the signal, "beguine." Porter noted that the rhythm so appealed to him that he jotted down the title "Begin the Beguine" in his notebook, returning to it a decade later—after his Kalabahi visit.

Jubilee opened 12 October at the Imperial Theater. Contrary to some later accounts, "Begin the Beguine"—as sung by June Knight and danced by her and Charles Walters—was not overlooked, in fact critics singled it out. Brooks Atkinson praised its "exotic originality"; others called it "alluring," "insinuating," "a honey." Much of its early impact beyond the show was due to Xavier Cugat, whose Latin-style band serenaded dancers nightly at the Waldorf-Astoria. Cugat played it often and recorded it alluringly for Victor.

One participant who had cause to remember "Begin the Beguine" was the great violinist Josef Gingold, concertmaster in the *Jubilee* orchestra. Supervising one of the early orchestral rehearsals, he announced to the assembled musicians, "All right, gentlemen. We'll now try the next number, 'Begin the Be-*guyn*' (to rhyme with 'fine')." All at once, he told Robert Kimball, "I felt a tap on my shoulder. There was this unassuming man, who simply said, 'Excuse me, but I think you'll find it's be-*geen*.' Of course it was Cole Porter. I never made that mistake again."

Then, too, there is the Robert Benchley story. "Why throw in just another rumba?" Porter remembered the actor-humorist saying to him shortly after *Jubilee* opened. Years later, Porter recalled, when the song had long since taken its place as an all-time standard, "Benchley used to hang out in a club on the Sunset Strip. Whenever I would walk in, the band would play 'Begin the Beguine.' Bob would hide his face behind a napkin and say, 'I know, I know.'"

Begin the Beguine
Artie Shaw and his Orchestra

The way Artie Shaw tells it, he recorded "Begin the Beguine" almost as an afterthought. His band had been in existence nearly two years, making records for Brunswick, without notable effect. At last, in mid-1938, Victor signed Shaw to its budget Bluebird label (35 cents a disc), and on 24 July the band turned up for its first date.

"The first record we made was a slambang version of Friml's old 'Indian Love Call,' with my old [Irving] Aaronson band colleague Tony Pestritto—now Tony Pastor—singing his own slambang version," Shaw wrote in his autobiographical *The Trouble with Cinderella*. "Everybody around the old RCA Victor studio thought we had a hit record. As it turned out the RCA Victor people were quite wrong. 'Indian Love Call' had an enormous sale; but that wasn't because it was a hit. It just happened to be on the other side of a rather nice little tune of Cole Porter's. . . . I had just happened to like it so I insisted on recording it at this first session, in spite of the recording manager, who thought it a complete waste of time and only let me make it after I had argued that it would at least make a nice quiet contrast to 'Indian Love Call.'"

Shaw's account does not quite match what Victor's files reveal—that his band recorded "Begin the Beguine" first, *before* they got to "Indian Love Call." And, too, there is alto saxophonist Hank Freeman's recollection that Shaw and Jerry Gray worked hard, well before the Bluebird date, to arrange "Begin the Beguine" in an appealing style.

"Artie and Jerry figured out a pulsating introduction which, in its way, was innovative," Freeman told historian Burt Korall. "In those days, intros were just intros, not a way to get things moving. And the intro, as you know, sold the tune."

Regardless of what happened in the studio, the Bluebird issue did indeed designate "Indian Love Call" as the "A" side. But it was "Begin the Beguine" that caught on from the first. "I joined the band three weeks after 'Beguine' became available in the stores," said trumpeter Bernie Privin. "Frankly, I didn't know too much about Shaw when I came over from Tommy Dorsey. But before I knew it, the band was the hottest thing in the country. The record was played everywhere. Because of it, Artie suddenly became a major celebrity."

Shaw's recording hit No. 1 on 15 November 1938 and remained there for six weeks. Save for its intro and coda, it consists simply of one full chorus, mostly ensemble, punctuated by brief solos from the leader's clarinet and Pastor's tenor sax. The national mania it created had its effect on Shaw, who felt himself a prisoner of his own popularity and ultimately bolted for Mexico one November night when he'd had enough, leaving his band leaderless on the stand at New York's Hotel Pennsylvania.

How far things went is apparent both from Porter's own 1944 effort, "Let's End the Beguine," and Noël Coward's devastating lines in "Nina":

She declined to begin the Beguine
Though they besought her to.
And in language profane and obscene
She cursed the man who taught her to.
She cursed Cole Porter too.

When Love Comes Your Way
Cole Porter

For Alec Wilder, this small charmer, one of *Jubilee*'s least known songs, may be more than it seems. "Could Porter possibly have been making a little fun of Noël Coward in 'When Love Comes Your Way'?" he asked in *American Popular Song*. "If he wasn't, it's hard to account for the existence of this song. It certainly has nothing to do with Porter, either in its lyrics or its music. And it is noticeably satirical, for it's an English music-hall waltz with every cliché in the book, plus a most pedestrian lyric containing such nuggets as 'Forget the world and say goodbye to sorrow' and 'Simply live for today and never think at all of tomorrow.' It had to be a pot shot."

And so it was, though a good-natured one. Porter wrote "When Love Comes Your Way" for the heavily Coward-inflected show *Nymph Errant*, and Gertrude Lawrence sang it in the pre-London tryouts until Porter replaced it with that 1933 show's title song. It resurfaced in *Jubilee*, sung by Derek Williams as the rather mannered English playwright Eric Dare, a broad caricature of Coward.

Nor is Coward the only public figure lampooned in *Jubilee*. The rather silly party-giver Eva Standing is clearly modeled on Porter's friend and quondam coconspirator Elsa Maxwell; and there are zingers for George Gershwin, including one related to his habit of monopolizing the piano at parties:

'Twill be new in ev'ry way,
Gershwin's promised not to play.

Even movie Tarzan Johnny Weissmuller turns up in the cast, thinly disguised as Charles Rausmiller, nicknamed "Mowgli," after the tree-swinging youth of Kipling's *Jungle Book*.

But the satire is far from apparent in the way Porter sings "When Love Comes Your Way" here. It is a small, even delicate, performance, and therein lies its considerable charm.

Why Shouldn't I?
Mary Martin

This Porter gem, also written during the 4 1/2-month *Franconia* voyage, can claim no origins in native dances or even *rive gauche* carryings-on. It is a straightforward love ballad, more than a little redolent of the unaffected simplicity of Irving Berlin, at least in its first half. But the way it unfolds is pure Porter, with a sophistication all the more remarkable because it never calls attention to itself.

Perhaps for that reason alone, "Why Shouldn't I?" almost got lost (as did "Just One of Those Things") amid the hoopla over the other *Jubilee* songs, notably "Begin the Beguine," "Me and Marie," and the obscure "The Kling-Kling Bird on the Divi-Divi Tree." It seems hardly believable that reviewer Robert Garland of the *Telegram* lamented that Porter's score contained "no whistling-as-you-walk-out melody ripe for one's pucker-up endeavors."

Martin's performance on this 1940 recording is as understated as the song itself. No Mermanian theatrics, no Libby Holman–style torchiness. She just sings the lyric in a straightforward and thoughtful way, her vocal quality buffed to a mellow luster.

Yet probably just because of this—and perhaps in an object lesson for some of today's more histrionic performers—she manages to put the message across with surprising poignancy. The sense of yearning, of love trembling on the brink, is almost palpable. It is a textbook example of "trust the song" (an adage well known to singers of "classic" pop), meaning that the minds or mind that fashioned melody and lyrics did so with great knowledge and care. The song is a world waiting to be explored.

That exploration does not require great embellishment, alteration, melodic distortion, textual liberty, or any of the other devices imposed by singers in the name of "interpretation." As Barbara Lea, whose work is represented elsewhere in this collection, put it in an interview with Whitney Balliett, "The song has to control the performance. Doing anything else—employing this or that trick—to make the audience applaud is an outrage. Then you are making them applaud *you*."

With simplicity and directness, Mary Martin serves "Why Shouldn't I?" very well indeed. As a contributor to George T. Simon's 1979 *The Best of the Music Makers* put it, "More than talent, more than just a strong soprano voice, personality, or natural stage presence, she had the ability to touch middle America at its most vulnerable point—its affection for the simple and sentimental. She was wholesome, spirited, feminine, and pretty, but not explicitly sexy; she projected family entertainment incarnate."

As she herself said in an interview, "I've never been jealous of a soul in my life. I've never been insecure. I love meeting people. I'm never nervous. I love to talk. I love to sing." And we will always love to listen.

Just One of Those Things
Louis Armstrong

As Moss Hart recalled it, Porter wrote "Just One of Those Things" precisely the way the movies portray songwriters writing songs: overnight, in a burst of divine inspiration. In August 1935, with *Jubilee* in tryouts, Hart and the Porters were taking a weekend's breather at the Ohio farm of Porter's Yale classmate Leonard Hanna. During a Saturday afternoon walk, Hart suggested that the second act was musically a little weak and could stand a major song. "I made a mental note that with luck we might have the song for the third week of rehearsal," he recalled.

Sunday morning, said Hart, he had not been out of bed long when Porter "called me into the living room and closed the doors. He placed a scribbled sheet of note paper on the music rack of the piano and then played and sang the verse and chorus of 'Just One of Those Things.' No word of either verse or chorus was ever altered. It has been played and sung through the years exactly as I heard it on that Sunday morning in Ohio, a song written overnight."

"Just One of Those Things" is one of the few Porter songs consistently favored by jazz instrumentalists; somehow its spare melodic line and almost stately chord sequence, spread across 64 bars, provide an inviting vehicle for creative improvisation in many styles.

Keyboard great Art Tatum seemed forever able to find new dimensions in it and recorded it several times in contrasting versions. A less likely admirer was New Orleans soprano sax pioneer Sidney Bechet, who played it often on club engagements (as he did "Love for Sale" and other Porter songs) and recorded it successfully in 1947. In the words of his protégé and admirer Bob Wilber, "It was a funny taste, perhaps, for a musician from New Orleans, but Porter's melodies, especially his juxtaposition of major and minor passages, seemed to fascinate Bechet."

Wilber's observation seems no less applicable to Bechet's coeval and fellow New Orleans–born jazz giant, Louis Armstrong. What is remarkable about this performance is not only the comfort with which Armstrong negotiates Porter's melody and lyric, but also the ease of his partnership with the trio led by virtuoso pianist Oscar Peterson. In 1957, when he made this record, Armstrong was fifty-six, separated from Peterson and his compatriots by two decades and an immense stylistic gulf.

To them, Armstrong must have represented a link with the very dawn of jazz history. This was the man, after all, who had recorded "Chimes Blues" with King Oliver in 1923, startled the music world with "West End Blues" in 1928, and transformed "Swing That Music" and "On the Sunny Side of the Street" in the 1930s. Yet here he was, backed by four musicians who were the toast of the "modern jazz" world, playing a show tune by a composer further removed from jazz than Harold Arlen, Hoagy Carmichael, or even George Gershwin or Irving Berlin.

Incongruous? Not a bit. Armstrong's performance is timeless, eternally contemporary. For Ray Brown, bassist on this and all the other Armstrong-Peterson dates, Armstrong "is the principal musician . . . the prime mover, the innovator. Everyone copied him . . . as Roy [Eldridge] said, 'Louis was the cat who laid it down.' I'll have to agree with that."

Small touches make this performance particularly memorable. The delight in his "Mama, jus' one of those craziest flings," or the second time round "just one of those nights," is quite contagious. And who could remain unmoved by the utter joy of Armstrong's delivery as he wraps things up with a final "So goodbye, dear, and a-men"?

His trumpet chorus, with Peterson and friends comping avidly behind him, has a spare majesty that any instrumentalist playing today could do well to emulate. Not a note placed wrong. Never an overbusy phrase. Just enough to set Porter's melody out in dazzling and inextinguishable lights.

Just One of Those Things
Bud Freeman and Bob Wilber

In one sense, the interplay of Bud Freeman's tenor sax with Bob Wilber's soprano on this lively performance has compositionally as much to do with Freeman as with Cole Porter. Of the three choruses heard here, one is a more or less straight melody statement, with the remaining two given over to variations on figures basic to Freeman's own style.

It is not an easy style to characterize. Some have described Freeman's whole approach to jazz improvisation as "serpentine." Others have called it "slithery" or even "slippery." Others have stressed its elegance and dry wit. It is all very subjective, but beyond argument Freeman's style owes little to either the ornamented romanticism of Coleman Hawkins or the light-toned understatement of Lester Young, long acknowledged as the two main paths of jazz solo development on tenor sax. A clue to Freeman's view of his own playing may be found in his titles for his various compositions: "The Sailfish," "Disenchanted Trout," "Margo's Seal," and, perhaps most famous of all, "The Eel."

Many characteristic figures, usually alternating triplets and short bursts of eighth notes, are part of the vocabulary on which Freeman and Wilber (himself a skilled arranger) draw in shaping "Just One of Those Things." Each man allows himself a 16-bar solo on the song's middle section, or bridge; but most of the number is ensemble, with brief solo openings toward the end for bassist Bob Haggart and drummer Gus Johnson.

The result is a performance that is clearly routined, but with figures that have been integral to Freeman's improvisational style since the 1920s. "Of course improvisation is always present in a jazz performance, to a greater or lesser degree," Freeman told Max Jones in a *Melody Maker* interview. "Improvisation is phrasing or rather, phrasing is improvisation. One note can be improvisation; it depends on what you want to do, and what you feel about a song."

BORN TO DANCE (1936 film)

Easy to Love
James Stewart

"I like it here," Cole Porter told columnist Dorothy Kilgallen shortly after his arrival in Hollywood to begin work on the score for MGM's blockbuster musical, *Born to Dance*. "It's like living on the moon, isn't it?" For him, at least, in a certain way it was. The way people did things and thought and the flamboyant but somehow primitive process in which major decisions were arrived at was new, quite different.

Throughout the first months of 1936 Porter kept a diary, recording in detail the responses of his bosses—including Irving Thalberg and the mighty Louis B. Mayer—to his work. The note concerning "Easy to Love," which he had originally written in 1934 for William Gaxton to sing in *Anything Goes*, was typical:

> The response was instantaneous. They all grabbed the lyric and began singing it, and even called in the stenographers to hear it, their enthusiasm was so great. When this singing was finally over, [dance director] Seymour Felix got on his knees in front of [executive producer] Sam Katz and said, "Oh please, Mr. Katz, let me stage that song when the picture is shot."

In a slightly later entry, Porter described the first casting discussions for *Born to Dance*. "After I returned home, I began thinking about James Stewart as a possibility for the male lead. I talked to Sam Katz about this on the telephone, and he thought the idea was most interesting, if Stewart could sing. The next day Stewart came over to the house and I heard him sing. He sings far from well, although he has nice notes in his voice, but he could play the part [of a clean-cut sailor] perfectly."

Stewart went ahead and recorded "Easy to Love" but got a rude shock when he saw *Born to Dance* for the first time. "I went to the preview," he told *New York Post* writer Martin Burden in 1988, "not feeling too secure about singing.... The picture came on—and it wasn't me singing. It was a fella who had a little bit of an English accent.

"But I understand that later the big boys in the limousines on the way back from the preview decided that the song, by Cole Porter, was so good that even I couldn't destroy it, so they put me back in." It is rather more likely that the composer, having auditioned and approved Stewart to do the singing, helped the studio bigwigs change their minds with a few well-chosen words of his own.

"I also remember very well," continued Stewart in his conversation with Burden, "they never asked me to sing in a movie again." Indeed, *Born to Dance* was the only film in which Stewart, the onscreen epitome of the shy, likable boy next door, sang. But as this extract from the soundtrack shows, he coped more than adequately with the task. His singing, while far from polished, has an engaging ardency, with—as Porter so precisely expressed it—some "nice notes in his voice."

Easy to Love
Judy Garland

"Roger Edens believed in Judy Garland," said Hugh Fordin during a conversation about the origins of this oddity, an MGM soundstage recording of Garland singing one of the major songs from *Born to Dance*. Virginia-born Edens had risen to Broadway prominence as pianist for George Gershwin's *Girl Crazy* and gone to Hollywood soon thereafter as Ethel Merman's accompanist. Endowed equally with charm and talent, he rose quickly to the position of musical supervisor at MGM.

In *The World of Entertainment*, Fordin identifies Edens as the soundstage pianist the day in 1935 that veteran vaudeville trouper Frank Gumm brought his twelve-year-old daughter Frances in to audition for Jack Robbins, then in charge of the studio's music-publishing division.

But songwriter Burton Lane, at that time a new presence on the Metro lot, insisted in a recent conversation that it was he at the piano when young Frances sang "Zing! Went the Strings of My Heart" and the popular Jewish liturgical piece, "Eli, Eli." Lane said he had heard the Gumm family performing between pictures at the Paramount Theater, phoned Robbins at home, and got him to set up the audition.

Whoever was at the keyboard, when the kid sang pandemonium broke loose. Within minutes, Arthur Freed—a songwriter then in the process of becoming a major producer—had summoned everyone of importance including Louis B. Mayer. The verdict: "She's going to be a big star."

But it took time. After doing a short, *Every Sunday*, with fellow hopeful Deanna Durbin, young Frances—now called Judy Garland—was considered briefly for *Born to Dance*, but was not used. All the while, Fordin wrote, "Edens' faith in Judy never wavered. He was fond of her and became her professional and personal adviser.... He coached her; he taught her to sing softly and from the heart; he dissuaded her from singing songs too sophisticated for a girl her age."

Edens had loved Porter's *Born to Dance* score, said Fordin, and thought "Easy to Love" a natural for Judy Garland to sing. "But there seemed no opportunity. They tried several versions over the years, and it became a favorite song of hers as well. But they never got it into a film." This recording represents one such attempt: it was intended for her to sing first in the 1938 film *Love Finds Andy Hardy*, and later in its

Frances Langford, Buddy Ebsen, Eleanor Powell, James Stewart, Virginia Bruce, and Sid Silvers in the film Born to Dance.

Frances Langford and the Foursome Quartet sing "Swingin' the Jinx Away" in Born to Dance.

1941 sequel, *Life Begins for Andy Hardy*, in which she starred with Mickey Rooney.

"Easy to Love" suited the Garland voice and temperament ideally; her performance here is heartfelt, full of a yearning quality that never loses its poignancy.

Easy to Love
Casper Reardon and his Orchestra

"The first and best of the short-haired harpists!" proclaimed *Metronome* magazine in an August 1937 article on Casper Reardon. "The man who made the cats forget the old theory that the golden strings are for spinsters only, and who was the first to prove conclusively that the harp can actually be swung."

The prose may have been inflated, but the claims for Casper Reardon seem to have been sound. His various appearances on record, whether as a sideman with Jack Teagarden in 1934 (his work on the trombonist's recording of "Junk Man" is notable) or as a leader of his own dates, show Reardon to be a remarkably flexible musician, a schooled and polished harpist who had also grasped the essentials of jazz and applied them to an unlikely instrument.

Harpist Daphne Hellman, whom Reardon replaced at Julius Monk's fashionable supper club Ruban Bleu, remembered him as "a very subtle player, kind of a musicians' musician. He played very softly, you know—of course in those days there was no way to amplify the harp, so it was always very soft. Lots of people, harpists, had that problem: Adele Girard, when she played with Joe Marsala at the Hickory House. Even Dorothy Ashby, who was pretty forceful.

"But Casper was different. He had this way of making everybody listen to him, concentrate on what he was doing. Something about the gentleness and finesse of his touch, I think. Really remarkable."

"Easy to Love" is from Reardon's last record date under his own name, made about a year before his death. It offers an arrangement—perhaps by the harpist himself—redolent of the intricate and imaginative writing Eddie Sauter had been doing for Red Norvo; the somewhat otherworldly vocal is by Loulie Jean Norman, whose clear high soprano later became an integral feature on records of songs by Kansas-born pianist-songwriter Willard Robison. There are two percussionists, one of them jazz drummer Chauncey Morehouse, with whom Reardon had recorded an album of original music by Dana Suesse, best known as composer of the pop standard "My Silent Love."

But the highlight of this performance is Reardon himself, his expansive melodic imagination and unfailing control of his instrument's dynamic possibilities. They make for rare and timeless music.

Rap Tap on Wood
Bobby Short

Cleveland newspaper columnist Winsor French had good reason to remember "Rap Tap on Wood," written for Eleanor Powell as part of Porter's *Born to Dance* score. Cole and Linda Porter had taken up residence at a luxurious Hollywood estate once owned by silent film star Richard Barthelmess. In addition to a swimming pool, tennis courts, and the rest of the trappings of filmland wealth, it had at least one sumptuously outfitted guest house; it was here that the Porters installed French and pianist Roger Stearns.

Porter, meanwhile, had taken avidly to Hollywood ways. Linda Porter did not share her husband's fondness for Southern California or the excesses of the film colony. The climate seemed to inflame her respiratory problems; movie folk held none of the fascination of the stars of the legitimate stage. From all reports she found the people coarse, the social drinking excessive, and much else wrong besides. But Cole seemed to thrive on it—particularly on the flattery of the studio heads—so she acceded to his enthusiasms.

Every evening around 10 P.M., French later wrote, Porter got to thinking about songs and would "drift toward the house I shared with Roger Stearns so they could sit down to the piano together and spin his latest brainchild into an endless duet. On one occasion, if anyone cares, I listened to 'Rap Tap on Wood' for not less than six hours."

Though the song proved to be a singing and dancing tour de force for Eleanor Powell, her all-stops-out performance missed the song's deliciously (and typically Porter) tongue-in-cheek quality. It is an affectionate spoof of all those manic smile-in-the-face-of-adversity ditties that Tin Pan Alley kept cranking out in the early days of the depression.

Bobby Short manages here to have it both ways. He revels in the high spirits, scattering prescriptions for happiness like a quack dispensing nostrums; yet he also makes interpretive common cause with Porter in having a bit of harmless laugh at the medicine man's expense.

I've Got You under My Skin
Lee Wiley

In 1954, nearly two decades after this record was made, columnist George Frazier wrote the following in a sleeve note to a Lee Wiley LP:

> In the not overwhelmingly genteel semantics of her own profession, Lee Wiley, a tall, striking-looking woman with olive skin, corn-colored hair and Cherokee blood, is "one bitch of a singer," which, for all its robustness, happens to be just about the sweetest, most terrific tribute

you can pay a person, meaning, as it so richly does, that he or she can reach your heart with her singing. In Miss Wiley's case—as heard by me anyway—it also means that she has a voice and style that have long since made me extremely eager to go to bed with her—but in a nice, noble way, you understand. For what I am getting at is that although she sings with devastating sex appeal, she does so in an exalted way. *(Courtesy of Festival Productions)*

The notes, predictably, created a small hurricane of controversy. Miss Wiley was said to have objected to Frazier's use of the word "bitch." The record company, fearful that such controversy might hurt sales, hastily backed down and sold copies of the album with a sticker over the offending paragraph, substituting blander sentiments than Frazier's.

But for all the brouhaha, Frazier was pretty much right on target. Miss Wiley's singing manages at most times to be both sensual and, to use the writer's word, exalted, and that emerges with stunning clarity in this performance. This was the period of the singer's close professional and personal association with the composer/violist-turned-leader Victor Young. Under his influence, the Oklahoma native had been studying voice, diction, elocution, and tackling a wider range of material on her regular radio programs.

Whatever she did, as Frazier said, she did with style. "About the vast art of Miss Wiley there is a sophistication that is both eloquent and enduring and utterly uncontrived.... Artistically, she's simply magnificent, projecting emotion with dignity and warmth, expressing nuances with exquisite delicacy, and always making you share her bliss or heartbreak."

Whether singing with her shoes off in a tight little studio with some jazz pals (see "Let's Fly Away") or accompanied, as here, by a no-expenses-spared radio orchestra, she comes across vividly.

I've Got You under My Skin
Cesare Siepi

In its original, undoctored form, "I've Got You under My Skin" has much in common with "Begin the Beguine." Both are lengthy songs, though this one at 56 bars cannot compete with the 108 of "Beguine"; both are unconventionally and irregularly structured, difficult to represent by the standard A-B-C thematic identifications; both develop serially, making them almost impossible to sing on any but their own, dramatic terms. Moreover, they share the sinuous, sensuous beguine rhythm, employ a wide vocal range, and present problems in conception and endurance for a singer.

Alec Wilder—even while confessing to a prejudice against such rhymes as "mentality" and "reality"—vouchsafes in his *American Popular Song* that "I've Got You under My Skin" is "so well composed and it develops its intensity and strength so remarkably as to demand acceptance."

Like "Begin the Beguine" and "In the Still of the Night," the song's long lines and aria-like phrase shapes have endeared it to opera singers in search of popular repertoire. None of the three has a verse, a fact that enhances the sense of each song as a straightforward bravura statement.

Some singers have succeeded in personalizing "I've Got You under My Skin" by abandoning both the declamatory manner of delivery and (as in the case of Frank Sinatra) the beguine rhythm. In Sinatra's celebrated recording, with discreetly swinging band accompaniment by Nelson Riddle, he does not so much sing the song as *confide* it, exposing various emotional levels in the lyric.

Cesare Siepi's approach is closer to the original, as sung in *Born to Dance* by Virginia Bruce: an open, expansive expression of helpless infatuation. Though technically a basso, he pitches the song in a relatively high key, fixing it firmly in the more sonorous bass-baritone range.

Swingin' the Jinx Away
Tempo King and his Kings of Tempo

No one who has seen *Born to Dance* will forget its all-stops-out finale, in which Eleanor Powell, backed by an extravagantly costumed chorus, sings and dances "Swingin' the Jinx Away" in front of what movie historian Roy Hemming has described as "a gleaming white battleship that could have been designed only by an art director whose heart was into Art Deco more than naval realism." So effective was the sequence that MGM lifted it entirely and reused it (wartime economy played a role here as well) as part of the World War II blockbuster, *I Dood It*.

But as Porter recalled in his Hollywood diary, "Swingin' the Jinx Away" almost fell prey to a jinx of its own. At first, MGM studio heads had loved it. "It went with a bang," Porter noted, "so my troubles are nearly over."

Less than a week later came a call from executive producer Sam Katz saying the finale—and with it the song—was out. "Everybody has decided the lyric is wrong and the tune doesn't have enough drive," said Katz. "Everybody" turned out to be mostly dance director Seymour Felix, who had other ideas about how the finale should go.

A stormy meeting resulted, and things looked grim—until Miss Powell herself got to her feet and announced, "Nobody has asked my opinion, but the number suits me perfectly. In fact I already have a routine which I would like to show you." She summoned her accompanist to the piano and went into what Porter remembered as "one of the most exciting dances I have ever seen in my life." As a result,

Jimmy Durante, Ethel Merman, and Bob Hope star in Red, Hot and Blue!

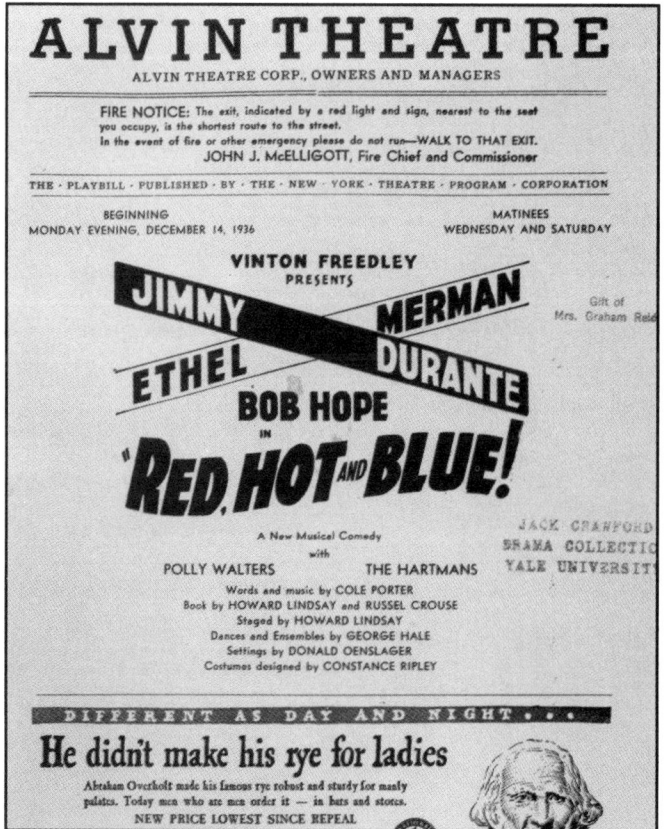

It was Porter's idea to crisscross the stars' names in The Playbill, *thereby solving the problem of who got top billing.*

"Swingin' the Jinx Away" stayed, Seymour Felix hit the road, and *Born to Dance* went on to be a major success, so much so that Louis B. Mayer promptly signed Porter to do another musical, and at a far higher salary.

If Tempo King's banishment of the "Jinx" is far in style from that lavish Hollywood production number, it is certainly no less spirited. Pianist Queenie Ada Rubin contributes some fancy swinging of her own to open things up, abetted by the brothers Marty (cornet) and Joe (clarinet) Marsala. It is probably not coincidental that the combination of her Waller-like piano and Tempo King's exhortations lends the whole performance a flavor redolent of the Fats Waller and His Rhythm records that were selling well for Victor at the time. A successful formula, after all, invites infinite replication.

Red, Hot and Blue! (1936)

Ridin' High
Benny Goodman and his Orchestra

In its original form, the show that became *Red, Hot and Blue!* was called *Wait for Baby!*, and as rehearsals began there must have been more than a few onlookers who found the original title eminently suitable. Everything, it seemed, was taking a back seat to a petulant feud between two agents, representing Ethel Merman and Jimmy Durante, over which star would get the coveted top left-hand billing on advertising.

That was only one of the headaches afflicting producer Vinton Freedley. The book was too long, and there were points at which Cole Porter's score fit awkwardly; the orchestral arrangements were uneven and needed work. On top of everything, Porter chose this time for a rare display of temperament. He had arrived late from Hollywood, having stopped off in Ontario to have a peek at the headline-making Dionne Quintuplets. When Freedley came at him with a list of proposed adjustments and changes, Porter became sullen and defensive.

The showdown came over the first-act finale. Robert Russell Bennett, the renowned orchestrator and an admirer of Porter's, felt that Merman's exuberant closer, "Ridin' High," was weak and needed revamping. He suggested alterations. Freedley, divining Porter's response, feared the worst.

He was right. Porter, hearing indirectly of Bennett's changes, hit the ceiling. He blamed Freedley. All the producer was doing, he complained, was carping unnecessarily. He shot off a telegram to Freedley, saying "I have lost all heart and stopped work." He requested that any further communication be through his lawyer, Dick Madden.

"Why can't he take it like a man and not hide behind your skirts?," Freedley stormed at Madden. "If he does not do something drastic"—and here, knowingly, he hit a Porter vulnerability—"he has another *Jubilee* to his demerit. Can he afford this?"

The shot had been accurate. Porter's self-confidence had taken a hammering with *Jubilee*'s relative lack of success; another near-disaster would be a potentially mortal blow.

Porter came around, doubtless with a strong assist from the harder-headed Madden. In a newfound spirit of cooperation, he also helped solve the Durante-Merman standoff by suggesting the names be crisscrossed on the billing, giving neither star an advantage over the other. He set to work with Bennett in adapting the score to the needs of book and staging. "Ridin' High," like everything else, worked out fine.

It also became one of the few Porter numbers of the period picked up by Benny Goodman. Where Artie Shaw seemed to regard Porter's unconventional structures and intricate melodies as a challenge, his clarinet-playing rival appeared to prefer simpler fare. With the exception of a Martha Tilton vocal on "In the Still of the Night," "Ridin' High" seems to be the only Porter number used by Goodman on radio or records during 1937.

The band played it as an instrumental on a 2 November *Camel Caravan* broadcast from the Madhattan Room of New York's Hotel Pennsylvania. And what an instrumental it is! Spurred by Gene Krupa's drumming, the band bites zestfully into a fast-moving Jimmy Mundy arrangement. Benny and Harry James trade 8-bar solos; note the roar that greets Harry's sizzling last effort—a vivid reminder of the popularity the twenty-one-year-old trumpet star had achieved after less than a year in Goodman's brass section.

Down in the Depths (on the 90th Floor)
Ethel Merman

The standard and oft-told tale behind this song goes roughly as follows: *Red, Hot and Blue!* is in the midst of its Boston tryouts. Preliminary reviews have been neither remarkably good nor distressingly bad (though Elinor Hughes of the *Herald* had suggested that there was enough libretto there for two shows). Porter is sulking; the big blowup over "Ridin' High" is soon to come. Ethel Merman, in the role of the indefatigable widow "Nails" O'Reilly Duquesne, needs a new number. Porter is reportedly working on it, though he has been so uncommunicative and contrary that no one knows what to expect.

One day at rehearsal, Porter is particularly withdrawn, reportedly walking by co-librettist Russel Crouse at least twelve times without even acknowledging him. Crouse is on the verge of asking whether he should change his toothpaste when Porter comes up to him, lays a friendly hand on his

Ensemble and five of the principals in Red, Hot and Blue!: *Vivian Vance, Jimmy Durante, Ethel Merman, Bob Hope, and Grace Hartman.*

Jimmy Durante as Policy Pinkle in Red, Hot and Blue!

shoulder, and says quietly, "in my pet pailletted gown." Shortly thereafter Porter presents the complete "Down in the Depths" to a grateful Merman.

Porter, talking to an interviewer a few days before the New York opening, declared matter-of-factly, "We all decided another song should be added. It had to be done in a hurry, of course, but I didn't have any difficulty, as I knew the situation in the show perfectly. I got my song in mind Tuesday, worked on it that night and Wednesday, and it was in the show, orchestrated, and sung by Ethel Merman on Thursday night."

Genesis aside, "Down in the Depths" fits the situation, and Merman, ideally. "When the incomparable Miss Merman sings a song," said Richard Watts in the *New York Herald-Tribune*, "she does it so magnificently that you immediately are lured into the belief that it is something of a masterpiece. It is only very careful second thought that leads you to the realization that it is something less than a classic."

Brooks Atkinson of the *Times* noted that "in Miss Merman's honor, Porter has scribbled off a few good songs [including] 'Down in the Depths of [sic] the 90th Floor,' where Miss Merman eats out her heart fortissimo . . . she is still the most commanding minstrel in the business, wearing her costumes like a drum major, swinging to the music and turning the audience into a congregation of pals for the evening."

Ours
Mabel Mercer

Among the few qualities Mabel Mercer and Lee Wiley had in common seemed to be an ability to kindle fires of passion in the ordinarily oh-so-urbane George Frazier. "Maybe I need an analyst or something," he wrote in his notes to a 1950s Mercer album, "but I am a man capable of falling in love three times a day." The object of his infatuation was a singer whose art came of an unerring ability to cut to the emotional heart of a song. A singer named Mabel Mercer.

"There is in this art an infinite sadness," he wrote, "and, I daresay, in us who respond to it a measure of masochism, because we are all, God wot, glad to be unhappy, oh, so very glad." In Mabel Mercer, moreover, he saw and heard the "quintessence of Manhattan"—though, God wot, a Manhattan that now belongs chiefly to history.

On its own, "Ours" is an elegant if somewhat unobtrusive song. It is little mentioned in the standard Porter biographies, overshadowed in discussions of *Red, Hot and Blue!* by such star turns as "Down in the Depths" and "It's De-lovely." But "Ours" delivers its own sneak punch with surprising power. It is an exhortation, rather quiet, that says, "How silly we are to have let this thing between us go flat. Together we can still make it live, make it endlessly exciting."

In *Red, Hot and Blue!*, "Ours" was a duet, sung by Dorothy Vernon and Thurston Crane. The two lovers agree that they can recapture love's glories, but they differ as to how. He wants the glamour and intoxication of travel—the Riviera, the Arabian Sea, even sunshine on a Devonshire lawn. She finds the same excitement just by living life in New York—Broadway lights, a box at Madison Square Garden, a view of the East River from a Park Avenue penthouse.

It is all very adult, calling for restraint, affection, and a deep and generous humor. Which is just where Mabel Mercer comes in, bringing to bear an art at once subtle, refined, yet direct and emotionally true.

It's De-lovely
Mabel Mercer

Porter furnished two accounts of the genesis of "It's De-lovely," introduced memorably in *Red, Hot and Blue!* by Ethel Merman and Bob Hope. The setting of both versions is the 1935 'round-the-world cruise during which Porter and Moss Hart wrote *Jubilee*. In one, the liner *Franconia* is approaching Rio de Janeiro at daybreak; Cole and Linda Porter, having heard for years about the glories of a Rio sunrise, are determined to see one. "My wife and I had risen especially for the event," he told an interviewer years later. "But Mr. Woolley had stayed up all night to see it and during the night had enjoyed a few whiskey-and-sodas. As we stood on the bow of the boat my exclamation was, 'It's delightful!' My wife followed with 'It's delicious!' And Monty, in his happy state, cried, 'It's de-lovely!' This last exclamation gave me the title for the song."

Version two sets the scene on the far side of the globe. "I was in Java with Monty Woolley and Moss Hart," he recounted later. "We'd just been served that famous Eastern fruit, the mangosteen, and were all enjoying it mightily. . . . Moss Hart said, 'It's delightful!' I chimed in with 'It's delicious.' And Monty Woolley said, 'It's de-lovely!' and there's the title for the song."

Whatever its origins, "It's De-lovely" is a song of good humor and infectious high spirits, following a relationship from its inception ("You can tell at a glance/What a swell night this is for romance/You can hear dear mother nature murmuring low,/'Let Yourself Go'"), through marriage ("How they cheer and how they smile/When we go galloping down the aisle"), honeymoon, the birth of their first child and, finally, the golden moment when "Our boy grows up, he's six foot three,/He's so good looking he looks like me."

It can be sung simply with enthusiasm, as a paean to "the riddle of married life," and it will work just fine, as countless performers have discovered. Then, too, it can be sung as Mabel Mercer sings it here, with just a hint of laughter some-

Tony Pastor sings "Rosalie" with Artie Shaw and his Orchestra in 1939.

The Ray Noble Orchestra in London in the 1930s. Al Bowlly is seated on the floor.

where behind the voice. The effect is—well, delicious: it is as if she is both singing the words and standing a step or two back from them, chuckling with affection at the eternal comedy being played out before her.

Both Woolley's catchphrase and the song it inspired were soon absorbed into the mainstream of contemporary American speech. Echoes and parodies became—and still are—commonplace. The very week in which these notes are being written, in the final decade of the twentieth century, the *Village Voice* (a publication far removed from everything Cole Porter stood for), runs a headline that reads, "It's DeKooning, It's Debuffet, It's Degrading."

Rosalie (1937 film)

Rosalie
Artie Shaw and his Orchestra

Back in Hollywood on the $100,000 salary he had won from MGM after *Born to Dance*, Porter set to work on a score for *Rosalie*. Things seemed to be going well, until he was asked to play through the score for Louis B. Mayer. Each tune got a nod of approval; but when Porter finished breezing through the film's title song, Mayer darkened, "Too highbrow," he growled. "Forget you're writing for Nelson Eddy and just give us a good popular song."

Beneath his customary urbanity, Porter was furious. He had already labored over, and discarded, five versions of "Rosalie" in search of a number that would be strong enough to carry the film's title. Now, having finally arrived at one he liked, he had to jettison it and start again—on what? "A good popular song"?

"I took 'Rosalie no. 6' home," he wrote in his diary, "and in hate wrote 'Rosalie no. 7.'"

Mayer, of course, loved it. It was simple, straightforward, conventional (it bears a passing resemblance to the 1919 music-hall favorite, "That Naughty Waltz"), eminently hummable. And, once the movie got into circulation, it was an instant hit. Even if Porter wrote the worst song he could out of contempt for what he surely viewed as Mayer's Philistine tastes, "Rosalie no. 7" was an undeniable success.

Irving Berlin advised him to "never hate a song that has sold a half-million copies," and Porter's friend and confidant Dr. Albert Sirmay said years later that he had heard all seven versions of "Rosalie" and that no. 7 was by far the best.

"I agree with Porter," said Artie Shaw, never a man to shrink from controversy, in a recent conversation. "It was a silly song. But it was direct and simple—so simple you could do things with it. The chief appeal of songs in a swing band context, I think, lies in what you can do with them. We had fun with 'Rosalie.' That's why I had Tony [Pastor] sing it. He had no voice to speak of, just that earnest, almost soprano version of a Louis Armstrong sound. But it was fun."

Shaw laughed as he got further into the reminiscence. "Thinking about Tony Pastor, I remember Frank Sinatra coming up to me once and begging me for a job. He was on the outs with Tommy [Dorsey]. He said to me, 'Why don't you put on a boy singer?' I gestured at Tony and said, 'I've got a boy singer.' He said, 'You call him a singer?' I said 'Yeah—he makes me laugh.' And that was the end of it."

This "Rosalie" arrangement, said Shaw, "was a real patch job, mostly put together in the recording studio: you know, jump from letter 'A' to letter 'G,' then back to 'B.' That kind of stuff. Listen to that little modulation I play with just the rhythm section to get us into the vocal. That was made up on the spot. And you know," he paused, "I thought I played a pretty interesting half-chorus solo on that one."

In the Still of the Night
a) Al Bowlly
b) Jessye Norman

Once a legend has been around awhile, there comes a point at which whether or not it is true is no longer of cardinal importance. Did Louis B. Mayer *actually* cry when Cole Porter played and sang "In the Still of the Night" for him? Maybe so, maybe not. The important thing is that he *could* have. And that this long, elegiac ballad from *Rosalie* is the kind of direct and unadorned statement that could—and did—reach the hearts of millions of people no more sophisticated than the MGM founder and boss.

Curiously, it almost did not get the chance. According to most accounts, Nelson Eddy, star of *Rosalie*, did not like it. At 72 bars, he said, it was too long. Its 16-16-24-16 bar structure made it something of a test of vocal endurance, with its big climax in the middle and half the song yet to sing. As tactfully as he knew how, Eddy let Porter know he did not want to sing it; would the composer consider writing something else in its place?

Porter dug in his heels. He would let Mayer be the judge. And "L. B.," as he was called, quickly made it known that Eddy would sing "In the Still of the Night," and that was that. Not surprisingly, Eddy wound up loving the song and made it a part of his standard concert and radio repertoire, to great acclaim, for the rest of his career.

It is an unabashedly sentimental song with more than a little of the aria to it, just as there was to "I've Got You under My Skin." It is clearly that aspect—the broad sweeps of melody, the long, legato phrases, and slightly stagy climax of the middle section—that worked for Nelson Eddy and has endeared "In the Still of the Night" to several generations of opera singers venturing into popular repertoire.

Its heart-on-sleeve directness is also ideally suited to the emotional crooning of Al Bowlly, who sings it here with almost palpable tenderness. Listening to him, it is easy to believe Ray Noble's recollection that "when he sang a love lyric it really got him.... I've seen him sing at the mike in front of the band, and there've been tears in his eyes as he turned away after finishing."

As the fashionable London magazine *Ideas* described a Bowlly performance in 1933: "With his lips a bare three inches from the microphone, he sings softly, confidently—and more people thrill to his voice than to Mussolini's and Hitler's put together."

Bowlly's romantic singing and dark good looks assured him no dearth of female admirers. According to colleagues, women chased him with often fanatical determination; at one point several reportedly competed for his favors by sewing and sending to him ever more original and audacious pieces of underwear, all of which he allegedly wore. One rapturous fan wrote to him that, "When your voice comes on the air, it's just like fizzy lemonade being poured down my spine!"

Jessye Norman's approach to the song is less involved than Bowlly's, but her tonal splendor and personal magnetism more than compensate. A listener may remain outside the textural and emotional life of the song, but intensity of delivery, coupled with sheer vocal excellence, creates its own emotive force as Norman carries "In the Still of the Night" from the faintest pianissimo to an exuberant fortissimo climax.

I've a Strange New Rhythm in My Heart
"Art Shaw and His New Music"

"I've always liked this record," Artie Shaw said in a recent conversation. "Remember, we were first and foremost a dance band, and this tune, arranged this way, was a good opener for a set. In fact there were many evenings when we'd open the night with it. Got 'em in the mood, got 'em dancing. A good, straightforward non-tricky presentation of an interesting tune, all with a good, solid beat."

An unusual highlight of this recording is the 16-bar "scat" vocal in the middle by Leo Watson, who at the time was appearing on 52nd Street as a member of the vocal-instrumental quintet, the Spirits of Rhythm. Their performances were a kind of controlled insanity, setting rhythmic, often manic and wildly imaginative vocals against a solid beat laid down on one standard guitar, three tiples (miniature guitars), and drums.

"I liked Leo very much," said Shaw. "He was a nutty little guy. I liked him musically and I liked him personally. I said, 'C'mon up and do the date. We'll figure out something for you to do.' He wound up on three things: 'Shoot the Likker to Me, John Boy,' 'Free Wheeling,' and this one.

"I showed him the arrangement and said, 'There's a 16-bar slot in here. All you have to do is listen to us play it and then do whatever with it you want....' Leo sang it in that way of his, and I thought it turned out just great. Still gives me a kick."

You Never Know (1938)

At Long Last Love
Lena Horne

Of all Cole Porter shows, *You Never Know* was arguably the least notable. Porter himself judged it an "immense flop," and critics and audiences hastened to agree. It closed after a mere seventy-eight performances, supplanted at the Winter Garden Theater by Olsen and Johnson's long-running and extravagantly successful *Hellzapoppin'*. Its only legacy to the canon of outstanding Porter songs is "At Long Last Love."

The story surrounding "At Long Last Love," closely bound up with the riding accident that changed Porter's life, is hazy. According to most accounts, he lay on the ground after his fall while help was summoned. "When the horse fell on me, I was too stunned to be conscious of great pain," he told an interviewer some time later. "But until help came I worked on the lyrics for a song called 'At Long Last Love.'"

It makes an appealing picture: the injured Porter lying there with pencil and paper in hand and keeping agony at bay with "Is it the good turtle soup or merely the mock?" But fact has an awkward way of disrupting such idylls. On 6 October 1937, eighteen days before the accident, "At Long Last Love" was registered for copyright as an unpublished song.

What is going on here? Was Porter's story, as Benny Green suggests, simply a fabrication, "a recourse to self-advertisement"? It is worth bearing in mind that "At Long Last Love" is, strictly speaking, one of Porter's "list songs." Like "You're the Top," its lyrics are an inventory of otherwise unconnected items collected to prove a point. In "You're the Top" it was simply everything considered the very best in the context of 1934. "At Long Last Love" sets up contrasts—plain vs. handsome, tawdry vs. elegant, low kitsch vs. high art. It is quite plausible that the version of the song registered for copyright on 6 October had a fully formed lyric in place, but that Porter, as was his wont, could not stop thinking up new and clever couplets and working them into the text.

Mary Martin made her Broadway debut in Leave It to Me, *1938.*

In support of the work-in-progress hypothesis, Robert Kimball points out that as late as 18 February 1938, a month before its publication, "At Long Last Love" still lacked a verse. Further, as first sung by Clifton Webb during the long pre-Broadway tryout period of mid-1938, the line that became "Is it Granada I see or only Asbury Park?" was in the second refrain and read "Is it the Lido I see or only Asbury Park?" It was later moved to the first refrain, replacing "Will it be Bach I shall hear, or just a Cole Porter song?" Finally, too, the last refrain, beginning, "Is it in marble or is it in clay?," remains unfinished to this day.

In other words, the fiddling and adjustment process never stopped, not even as Porter lay on the ground and held off the pain in his own way.

Lena Horne's 1958 recording works effectively on two emotional levels. On the surface, all is delight and surprise at having finally found the "real McCoy," the long-sought and often all too elusive satisfactions of love. But not too far down is another layer, with strong undertones of anger and frustration. Why did it take so long? Why did I have to go through so many false starts? Why didn't I find this *sooner*, instead of—in Cole Porter's apt phrase—wasting precious time?

It is a combination of emotions close to Lena's own, after a life of frustrations and near-victories before the great paroxysmal triumph of *A Lady and Her Music* on Broadway in 1981. Perhaps for this reason alone, her reading of "At Long Last Love" is deeply convincing; how reassuring to think that Lena Horne at last found her own "real McCoy."

She is backed here by an all-star New York studio band, including such standouts as trumpeters Bernie Glow and Jimmy Maxwell, trombonists Frank Rehak and Eddie Bert, and the great bassist George Duvivier, who was part of Lena's regular rhythm section at the time. "She was like one of the guys," Eddie Bert remembered in a recent conversation. "She'd hang out with us, knew what was happening. We'd met some years before at Cafe Society, when I sat in with Red Allen and J. C. Higginbotham and she was on the bill. I'd thought at the time that she was a regular chick. That never changed: we always had a ball. The record dates went easy—like a party. Fantastic."

The Sun Never Sets (1938)

River God
Todd Duncan

This is a curiosity among Porter songs. Its subject matter, treatment, atmosphere, and emotional thrust are far removed from the world of "You're the Top" or "Begin the Beguine." Heard for the first time, it sounds like what might have resulted had Porter, rather than Jerome Kern, set out to write a major "river song" for *Show Boat*.

Perhaps that explains why it is all but unknown even among Porter admirers. It is an anomaly, written as an assignment and slotted into a British show, which later became a film. It bears no "typical Porter" hallmarks, no witty turns of phrase or little melodic touches. Yet it remains a strong and memorable piece of work.

In March 1938 Porter's old associate Guy Bolton sent him a script he had written in collaboration with Pat Wallace, son of the great and prolific English novelist Edgar Wallace (1875–1932). Titled *River of Stars*, it was based on some Edgar Wallace stories set in West Africa. In one, the hero prepares for a voyage up the river Congo. Could Porter, Bolton asked, fashion a song that would capture the momentousness of the undertaking, the majesty of the river, and the man's deep determination in embarking on so long and perilous an adventure?

Perhaps in a spirit of challenge, Porter agreed. In characteristically thorough fashion he set about the necessary homework, which included compiling long lists of indigenous African animals. He completed "River God" a month later, dating his manuscript—a practice he had adopted after the accident—4 April 1938.

River of Stars, retitled *The Sun Never Sets*, opened at London's Drury Lane Theater on 9 June 1938, with a cast that included *Blackbirds* veteran Adelaide Hall and, perhaps looking ahead to his characterization of Allan Quartermain in *King Solomon's Mines*, a youthful Stewart Granger.

If *The Sun Never Sets* is remembered now for anything, however, it is for Todd Duncan as the voyager, delivering Porter's "River God" in his deep, resonant baritone. Duncan was already something of a celebrity through his portrayal of Porgy in the original 1935 production of *Porgy and Bess*. Teacher at Howard University, holder of a Master's degree from Columbia, and trained as a concert singer, he came to *The Sun Never Sets* after an acclaimed performance in Mascagni's *Cavalleria Rusticana* in New York.

Perhaps "River God" is overblown, stagy, and as full of labored sententiousness as some have suggested. But the strength and simple power of Duncan's performance quite transcend such considerations.

Leave It to Me (1938)

My Heart Belongs to Daddy
Mary Martin, with Eddy Duchin and his Orchestra

Cole Porter had a lot riding on *Leave It to Me* when it opened at New York's Imperial Theater on 9 November 1938.

The cast at the curtain call of Leave It to Me, *1938.*

Mary Martin sings "My Heart Belongs to Daddy" in Leave It to Me. *To her immediate right is Gene Kelly, who also made his Broadway debut in the show.*

Rosemary Clooney in 1953.

Though *Jubilee* and *Red, Hot and Blue!* had contained some fine songs, they had been, relatively speaking, box-office disappointments. *You Never Know,* coming next, had lasted only seventy-eight performances and was, said Porter, "the worst show with which I was ever connected."

His recent fortunes in the movies were not much better. Compared to the high praise heaped on *Born to Dance, Rosalie,* for all Louis B. Mayer's enthusiasm, had turned out to be, in historian Roy Hemming's words, "one of the dullest, drippiest, most overproduced spectacles that MGM or anyone else made in the '30s." Seen from that perspective, Porter's disabling accident could not have come at a worse time. All circumstances seemed to have conspired to sap his last ounce of self-confidence.

Outwardly he appeared to take it all with good grace. But those close to him knew that without some new triumph, some reaffirmation that the Cole Porter of *Anything Goes* was still alive and functioning, he might well be professionally washed up.

The hoped-for reversal of fortune came with *Leave It to Me*, and to a great extent because of an elfin bundle of Texas energy named Mary Martin. In the edited vocal excerpt heard here she briefly recounts the circumstances of her audition for a roomful of theater notables.

She remembered Porter saying she had been "divine." But as playwright Bella Spewack said later, "He always said 'divine.' I didn't know whether he meant it." Porter himself recalled the newcomer as "a dreary little girl who appeared to be the last word in scared dowdiness." That was before he heard her sing all four songs she had prepared. Thereafter, he avidly described those few moments as "the finest audition I had ever heard."

Mary Martin doing "My Heart Belongs to Daddy" was nothing short of a sensation. She appeared onstage as Dolly Winslow, a young American stranded at a Siberian railroad station, clad only in a white shortie fur coat. She accompanied the suggestive lyric with a mock striptease that, however demure, brought down the house and fetched a complaint in print from Boston's eternally prim Elinor Hughes.

Until the day she died, Mary Martin insisted that when she first sang "My Heart Belongs to Daddy" she had been too naive to understand its obvious sexual innuendo. Perhaps she was. But the very sense of innocence she brought to her delivery seemed to emphasize the double entendre of such lines as,

> If I invite
> A boy some night
> To dine on my fine finnan haddie,
> I just adore
> His asking for more,
> But my heart belongs to Daddy.

Listening to the melody, particularly its cantillated "da-da-da, da-da-da, da-da-da" middle section, brings to mind Richard Rodgers's account of his first meeting with Porter in Venice in 1926. They got into a discussion of their shared craft, and Porter explained that in his view a surefire way to succeed as a songwriter was to "write Jewish tunes." At first Rodgers laughed—until it occurred to him that his companion was serious.

Was he? At this remove it is hard to tell, even though some of Porter's most enduring melodies have about them certain qualities (particularly in their balance of major and minor tonalities) that could be called "Mediterranean" or even "Jewish." Rodgers seems to have accepted it, as remarks in his autobiography *Musical Stages* confirm. Alec Wilder, too, seems to believe it and mentions in *American Popular Song* that "the melody disturbs me in its implication . . . that 'Daddy' is Jewish. I find the inside humor in this song in poor taste." Many, notably Porter historian Robert Kimball, find Wilder's opinion unfounded.

Get Out of Town
Rosemary Clooney

By the time *Leave It to Me* opened on Broadway, the world was in what Will Rogers, had he lived, might have called "one hell of a mess." Hitler had annexed Czechoslovakia, and Neville Chamberlain had returned from Munich with his fragile "peace in our time." In Spain, Franco's loyalists were pushing back Republican forces; Japan was on the march in China; and Stalin's show trials and purges were making a mockery of the Soviet Bolshevik revolution. At home, Texas Democrat Martin Dies became chairman of the newly formed House Un-American Activities Committee.

Yet here was an obviously light-hearted political farce that managed to send up just about everybody in one way or another. Only a decade before, the political satire *Strike Up the Band* was rewritten because its book, which pilloried war profiteering, jingoism, and diplomatic hypocrisy, was considered too controversial for Broadway audiences.

Times had changed. When Victor Moore, as mild-mannered businessman Alonzo P. Goodhue, kicks a goose-stepping Nazi ambassador in the belly during *Leave It to Me*, Franklin D. Roosevelt's Secretary of State Cordell Hull sends congratulations—and the audience cheers right along with him.

The book, by Sam and Bella Spewack, is full of well-aimed zingers, and few prominent figures are spared. As the first act closes, "Stinky" Goodhue, now United States Ambassador to Moscow, is feted in Red Square as a hero of the Revolution. His wife (played by the ebullient Sophie Tucker) exclaims, "I'll bet the Kennedys are boiling," a broad reference to the virulent anti-communism (and reputed Nazi sympathies) of Ambassador to Britain Joseph P. Kennedy.

Leave It to Me closed in mid-1939 but was so popular that it was revived briefly later that year. By that time, World War II was under way, and changes were necessary. The character of "Uncle Joe" Stalin, who had danced a jig (to the Communist "Internationale") in honor of Goodhue during the Red Square celebration, was expunged. Goodhue's international "peace plan" was extensively revamped. And in case theatergoers still did not get the hint, a note was tucked into their playbills informing them that the show was not to be interpreted as a satire on world events.

The popularity of Mary Martin and "My Heart Belongs to Daddy" almost managed to obscure the equally worthy "Get Out of Town," sung in the show by Tamara, a beautiful Ukranian actress who had first won Broadway hearts in 1933 when she sang "Smoke Gets in Your Eyes" in Jerome Kern and Otto Harbach's *Roberta*. Most reviews, in fact, did not even mention it—a pity, as Alec Wilder indicates in *American Popular Song*, referring to "Get Out of Town" as "a very sophisticated, urbane and urban song."

Rosemary Clooney, whose latter-day career has included many composer tribute albums with jazz accompaniments, handles "Get Out of Town" in an engagingly rhythmic and straightforward way. Cornetist Warren Vache and tenor saxophonist Scott Hamilton contribute able solos.

Most Gentlemen Don't Like Love
Julie Wilson, with the Marshall Grant Trio

"This number is one of my all time favorites," Julie Wilson said of "Most Gentlemen Don't Like Love" in a recent conversation. "It's the perfect opening number. You know, [book writers] Sam and Bella Spewack were wonderful to me, treated me like their daughter. And they told me all sorts of stories about *Leave It to Me*, about Mary Martin and that short and sassy fur coat, and about Sophie Tucker, who introduced this number in the show.

"It's such a Sophie Tucker type of song. I wasn't fortunate enough to see her do it, but I'd met her and seen her in various clubs, and admired her wonderful sense of humor. When I found out she was the originator of the song on Broadway, I just thought, 'how perfect.'"

Miss Wilson laughed in mock astonishment. "The thing that always amazed me was that she never recorded it. Mary Martin did, and I remember thinking, 'Isn't she a clever girl, doing that?' You know, a song is like a little three-act play: casting it is so very important—the right person with the right song. The right age. The right style. So many songs work for one person and not another."

Had her own interpretation changed in the years since this 1957 performance of "Most Gentlemen?" "No. I don't think so. Once I fall in love with a song and get it in my gut a certain way, I rarely change it." Miss Wilson chuckled. "Well, maybe some of the innuendo gets a little—well, a little better, you know."

This performance was recorded live at the Maisonette Room of the St. Regis Hotel. "Those gentlemen [from RCA] just came in and said, 'We'd like to record you here,' and that was it. They recorded just one set, from beginning to end. No retakes, nothing. It all happened so fast. I was a kid then. I just forgot they were there and they did the show. You know how it is: there may be three people there, or 300—you just do what you do."

The Man Who Came to Dinner (1939)

What Am I to Do?
Hubbell Pierce

Cole Porter and Edgar Montillion Woolley had been friends since their undergraduate days at Yale. They met, appropriately, at a formal dinner, a banquet given by the campus *Yale News*, and soon discovered they shared many interests, chiefly a devotion to "the finer things" of life. Porter, in later years, was fond of saying, "All my life I've been accused of being a snob. I'm not: I simply like the best"; he could easily have been speaking for his friend Woolley.

As years passed and the Edgar fell away in favor of the more convivial "Monty," the two men remained close. Woolley was himself a talent, a deft, witty theater director who worked with Porter on *Fifty Million Frenchmen* and *The New Yorkers*. During the 1930s he was an indispensable part of Porter's life, whether watching the composer work out "Begin the Beguine" aboard the *Franconia*, perpetrating the high jinks that attended the birth of "Miss Otis Regrets," or proclaiming the glories of the Rio sunrise with the epithet, "It's de-lovely!" By all accounts, Woolley was great fun, unpredictable, and, in the slang of the day, quite a character.

He was also a capable actor. His portrayal of the bearded, irascible Sheridan Whiteside—a thinly disguised caricature of critic-essayist and Algonquin Round Table member Alexander Woollcott—in the George S. Kaufman–Moss Hart collaboration, *The Man Who Came to Dinner*, was an instant hit of the 1939–40 Broadway season.

Cole Porter's chief involvement in *The Man Who Came to Dinner* was with another character, the English playwright Beverly Carlton. Like Eric Dare in *Jubilee*, Carlton was a caricature of Noël Coward. Obligingly, Porter supplied him the very Coward-like "What Am I to Do?" to sing, and as if to underscore the parody, signed his manuscript "Noel Porter," much to Coward's reported amusement.

Hubbell Pierce delivers the song, and especially its opening verse, very much in that spirit. "Hubbell wasn't strictly speaking a professional musician," said William Roy, his accompanist on this recording. "But he knew all the songs, really adored them. He was very, very knowledgeable about Porter, and these songs—many of them things I never heard of—were very special to him."

Pierce, who made most of his living in interior decoration, recorded his Porter album as a fiftieth birthday present to himself. "He had 1,000 copies pressed up," Roy said, "and sent them around to his friends and others he thought would be interested. He'd come into some money, and was therefore able to get the best. The best people to record it, the best production. Quality all the way."

Partly as a result of this exposure, Pierce landed a job singing and playing the piano in the Birdcage, the small, glassed-in front room at Michael's Pub, a popular restaurant and supper club on East 55th Street. "He only played the piano in the key of C," said Roy. "And he didn't read music. I remember once teaching him the entire score to *Gypsy* in the key of C, which was probably the most tedious thing I've ever had to do.

"But he just heard stuff, and played what he heard. In the case of this record, he had a very clear idea of what he wanted to do. Picked all the material, routined it—and the recording went very easily, very fast. It *still* sounds awfully good to me."

BROADWAY MELODY OF 1940 (film)

I've Got My Eyes on You
Bob Crosby and his Orchestra

In early 1939 Porter was back in Hollywood to prepare a score for a new MGM extravaganza, at the time titled *Broadway Melody of 1939*. He seemed in good spirits and enthusiastic about the new film and set to work in his new beach house at Malibu.

"It was a small house," his friend Ray Kelly later recalled, "and although I thought I knew Cole well before, I got to know him even better there. In such confining quarters, I learned that he worked like a fiend, all hours of the day and night. A great many times I'd think I was talking to him and then suddenly it would dawn on me: he hadn't heard a word. He had music, or a lyric or something, going through his mind."

Though burdened with an implausible and utterly forgettable plot, *Broadway Melody of 1940*, as it ultimately came to be called due to a delay in its release, seemed to have a winning combination in Porter's music and Hollywood's two major dancing stars of the era, Fred Astaire and Eleanor Powell.

But surprises lay in store. The two dancers' styles were dissimilar almost to the point of incompatibility. Despite such outstanding new Porter songs as "I Concentrate on You" and "I've Got My Eyes on You," the movie's easy high point turned out to be the five-year-old "Begin the Beguine," featuring a nine-minute, four-part production number devised by Roger Edens and choreographer Bobby Connolly.

Notwithstanding their stylistic differences, there are moments in the sequence as good as anything either dancer ever put on film. The up-tempo tap routine toward the end, for example, survives as part of MGM's 1972 film compilation, *That's Entertainment*.

By Porter standards, "I've Got My Eyes on You" is pretty conventional stuff: just 32 bars long, structured in an easy ABAC, with a chord structure occasionally reminiscent of the composer's 1929 "You Do Something to Me." But, as Artie Shaw pointed out earlier, for just those reasons it lends itself nicely to the sort of jazz-based big-band treatment accorded it here by the Bob Crosby Orchestra.

Marion Mann's vocal is pleasant enough, but the real star of this performance is the Crosby orchestra. Its loose, dixieland-flavored ensembles exude a sunny buoyancy quite different from the tense energy of the other popular swing bands. The rhythm section, with its foundation in Ray Bauduc's broadly based drumming, harks back to New Orleans and the very roots of jazz. Eddie Miller, one of the most lyrical tenor saxophonists of the period, contributes a neatly turned 8 bars during the final chorus.

Please Don't Monkey with Broadway
Fred Astaire and George Murphy

To say the plot of *Broadway Melody of 1940* is flimsy understates the case. Down-on-his-luck Johnny Brett (Fred Astaire) coaches his pal King Shaw (George Murphy) well enough to land him a job as a dancing partner of Broadway star Clare Bennett (Eleanor Powell). Good reviews start coming in, and King shows himself to be a conceited ass; he gets drunk on opening night, and Johnny goes on for him at the last moment and is a sensation.

After many turns and improbable twists of situation, King finally realizes that Clare would rather dance—and be—with Johnny; he turns up at the theater, soused again, to announce he is leaving and his two friends had better get

Marion Mann with Bob Crosby's Orchestra at Chicago's Black Hawk Restaurant in 1938.

Fred Astaire and Eleanor Powell in Broadway Melody of 1940.

together. Exeunt all three, happily dancing "Begin the Beguine."

Unlikely? Absolutely. Yet it affords the three principals some fine opportunities for first-rate singing and dancing. "Please Don't Monkey with Broadway," for example, comes early in the film and teams Astaire with future California Senator Murphy, both in top hat, white tie, and tails, hoofing through one of the film's liveliest rhythm numbers. The two singer-dancers take good-natured swipes at Brooklyn, the Bronx, and other areas around New York City while praising the Great White Way. Then they wind up in a mock duel, using their canes as swords for some fancy swashbuckling.

It's all plenty exciting as Astaire and Murphy go through their onscreen paces. But the thrill of watching them comes from two separate sources. First it is the sound of the music and the energy and skill of their performance. Second, and no less compelling, is something a little more elusive. The poet Philip Larkin got close to it in a 1972 essay on Porter, observing that all of us, American or British, are forever "sneakingly impressed by the character in faultless clothes who can talk to French waiters and is with the best bunch on the beach." That is, a Porter. Or a Fred Astaire.

It is a variation on the same fantasy appeal that made Astaire's earlier films with Ginger Rogers such box-office smashes in the darkest days of the depression. As Arlene Croce put it in *The Fred Astaire and Ginger Rogers Book*,

> In the class-conscious Thirties, it was possible to imagine characters who spent their lives in evening dress . . . slipping from their satin beds at twilight, dancing the night away and then stumbling, top-hatted and ermine-tangled, out of speakeasies at dawn. It was a dead image, a faded cartoon of the pre-Crash, pre-Roosevelt era, but it was the only image of luxury that most people believed in.

This MGM sound track recording captures a lot of the *frisson* of that perception, while offering a liberal helping of honest-to-goodness upbeat music. It is also a rarity, in that it gives us the number and the entire routine *before* Astaire and Murphy overlaid their dancing. The result is a verse and two choruses of dual vocal, then three lively (and swinging) instrumental choruses by the studio orchestra, featuring some good, but uncredited, tenor sax and clarinet playing along the way. It might have been nice to know, half a century ago, the identities of those very capable soundstage players.

I Concentrate on You
Teddi King

On balance, many of the most memorable Porter songs seem to be those with extended lengths and irregular structures. Counting its "I concentrate and concentrate" coda, "I Concentrate on You" runs seventy-two bars, full of long, legato phrases and wide, handsome open spaces. It is easily the most enduring song to come out of *Broadway Melody of 1940*, and perhaps one of the composer's all-time best.

Curiously, it is used almost desultorily in the movie, with Eleanor Powell dancing at far from top form and Astaire joining her in what looks like equally half-hearted fashion while baritone Douglas MacPhail does the singing.

But "I Concentrate on You" continued to win friends and impress listeners long after *Broadway Melody* faded from the nation's screens, partly due to its remarkable flexibility. It can be sung in several ways, each with its own emotional tone and flavor. Some singers choose to regard it as an upbeat, joyous affirmation of belief in the restorative power of a love affair. "Whenever skies look gray to me/And trouble begins to brew," it says, I simply think about you and all is immediately well.

But "I Concentrate on You" can just as readily be an expression of despair, a last-ditch cry of fading hope. In this projection, the singer may have lost her (or his) loved one; all is doubt, even dread. "When Fortune cries, 'Nay, nay!' to me/And people declare, 'You're through'" can reflect a dogged hold on the memory of a time when love's bliss could weather any crisis.

And, too, there is an emotional middle ground, more elusive for a performer, but perhaps ultimately most satisfying. In this interpretation the singer is alone, perhaps threatened by circumstances, but able to derive strength from the knowledge that love's flame still burns quietly and steadily within.

It is this vision that lies at the heart of Teddi King's evocative reading of "I Concentrate on You." John McLellan Fitch, who produced the 1953 session, remembered her performance well: "There was something about the way she sang a ballad that could really grab you," he said in a recent conversation. "I was just bowled over by that voice. I thought she was the best ballad singer I'd ever heard; I still can't think of anybody, with the possible exception of Ella [Fitzgerald] or Sarah [Vaughan], who could do so well with this sort of song."

Fitch, who was working at the time for Boston radio station WHDH-AM under the name John McLellan, recorded the ten-inch LP for George Wein's Storyville label, at Wein's Boston club of the same name. "We did it late at night, after the club had emptied," Fitch recalled. "I simply brought an engineer from the station and set up a portable machine.

"It's funny. I'd had no idea until it got really quiet in there how squeaky the piano was, how much noise there was on the stage, in the room. It wasn't a professional sound studio by any means. But things went fairly easily: no real problems, and certainly no more than two takes per number.

"And Teddi." Here he paused, in momentary contemplation. "You know, I can hear that voice even now, and it still stops my heart. Whether it's the purity, or that distinctive fast vibrato, her diction—I don't know what. Whatever it is, it's just mind-boggling."

Du Barry Was a Lady (1939)

Friendship
Judy Garland and Johnny Mercer

As December of 1939 began, all the news was bad: Great Britain was at war with Nazi Germany and bringing increasing pressure on the United States to enter the conflict. President Franklin D. Roosevelt resisted, holding to a scrupulous neutrality—at least on paper. But to Edward R. Murrow, reporting from London, it looked more and more as though "we are all passengers on an express train traveling at high speed through a dark tunnel toward an unknown destiny . . . the suspicion recurs that the train may have no engineer . . . no one who can bring us to a standstill."

At home the lights of Broadway still glowed brightly as 1939, and the decade with it, went out in extravagant and high-kicking style. Nothing typified it better than *Du Barry Was a Lady*, opening 6 December at the 46th Street Theater. Both for the Broadway stage and for Cole Porter, it was an unalloyed triumph.

Its story was a convoluted and far-fetched affair about a washroom attendant who swallows a Mickey Finn and finds himself back in the court of the weak and foolish French King Louis XV. However improbable, it provided a vehicle for one of Porter's most inspired scores, for the comic talents of Ethel Merman and Bert Lahr, and for a newcomer to the stage—a pint-sized Hollywood bombshell named Betty Grable.

There was, in historian Stanley Green's words, "nothing new or novel about *Du Barry*. Just a big, splashy, slickly put together show, featuring two of the stage's most outstanding musical-comedy performers . . . and songs by one of its most renowned composers." Its tone seemed to be just what the doctor ordered: low comedy all the way, replete with off-color jokes and, in Porter's case, risqué song lyrics. In all, many felt, an evening perhaps closer to Burlesque than to Broadway.

Critical response was mixed. Brooks Atkinson of the *Times*, while conceding that Porter "had written a number of accomplished tunes in the modern idiom," sniffed that the lyrics were "no more inspired than the book." But for the veteran *Newsweek* critic George Jean Nathan, *Du Barry* was "a frankly and brazenly vulgar show from the start to finish, full of lavatory, boudoir and posterior gags . . . [and] good for a lot of loud low laughs."

More than a few guffaws attended "Friendship," which provided an ideally bantering vehicle for the show's two comic stars. Producer B. G. (Buddy) De Sylva, no mean songwriter himself, had asked Porter to write something with "low-level sentimental appeal." Porter went him one further and turned out this bit of *faux*-hillbilly tomfoolery. Like "At Long Last Love," it is a Porter "list" song; not surprisingly, the composer seemed forever to be coming up with new couplets, sometimes added moments before curtain time.

During tryouts in Boston, New Haven, and Philadelphia it was a smash. On one occasion, George Eells reported in his Porter biography, *The Life That Late He Led*, an audience demanded so many encores that Lahr and Merman wound up trooping back onstage clutching sheets of paper on which new lyrics had been hastily typed.

New York was another matter, at least on opening night. Whether it was the tune's Ma-and-Pa-Kettle flavor or what Brooks Atkinson termed its "slatternly" lyrics, Manhattan first-nighters seemed none too friendly to "Friendship." Porter stood his ground, and second-night response seemed to vindicate his faith. *Du Barry* played to ninety-eight standees Saturday night of opening week and by the following weekend was outgrossing (perhaps in both senses) any other show in town.

By April, "Friendship" was enough of an established hit for Judy Garland to work up as a duet with Bob Hope for one of the comedian's regular Tuesday night Pepsodent radio shows. On the day between dress rehearsal and the broadcast she recorded it with another partner, songwriter-singer Johnny Mercer, and with salutary results: the chemistry was good, the sense of fun infectious. On this alternate take, which lay in Decca's vaults until its release in 1980, Garland goofs the lyric that should read, "If they ever black your eyes, put me wise." Her little chuckle, as she realizes what she's done, is a piquant and endearing touch.

Do I Love You?
Ella Fitzgerald

George Jean Nathan, never one to mince words, thought he heard something and told the world about it. After attending the opening night of *Du Barry Was a Lady*, he commented in *Newsweek* that "Mr. Porter's big song hit, 'Do I Love You?,' may find you simultaneously whistling 'It's a Long Long Way to Tipperary' without anyone's being any the wiser."

As a friend and collaborator of H. L. Mencken, cofounder of *The Smart Set* and a highly regarded man-about-literary-affairs, Nathan was not to be taken lightly. But readers comparing "Do I Love You?" with "Tipperary" were hard-pressed to hear the resemblance he had noted. Porter finally

Bert Lahr and Betty Grable in Du Barry Was a Lady.

Helen Forrest in the early 1940s.

dismissed the whole matter, perhaps a trifle irreverently, with a full frontal assault on the veteran critic's musical acumen. "George Jean Nathan," he declared, "wouldn't recognize 'The Star-Spangled Banner' unless he saw everyone else standing up."

What was beyond dispute was that *Du Barry* was a hit, running for a whopping 408 performances, and that Porter had at last regained his old form. Viewed in retrospect, it now seems less a great show (Porter's songs excepted) than an eminently timely one. Events in Europe were moving forward with a terrible swiftness, as the Nazi war machine spilled over into Denmark, Norway, Belgium, Luxembourg, and Holland. The British, overpowered and outflanked, withdrew at Dunkirk. By June, France fell to the Germans, who established a puppet government at Vichy under Marshal Pétain. In London, newly elected Prime Minister Winston Churchill, addressing the House of Commons, offered his beleaguered countrymen little save "blood, toil, tears and sweat."

No wonder the laughter at the 46th Street Theater was just a little strident. As Charles Schwartz put it in his Porter biography, it is "perhaps easy to see why the show's boisterous, bawdy humor was such a delightful palliative for the crowds who flocked to see it."

"Do I Love You?" was sung in the show by Ethel Merman, of whom Arturo Toscanini once said, "she does not possess a voice but another instrument in the band." Ella Fitzgerald, by contrast, has a voice to gladden the ear and uses it to telling effect in this performance. The song is an ideal vehicle for her: emotionally open, straightforward, uncomplicated, a single heartfelt sentiment borne aloft on the gossamer wings of a graceful melody.

When Love Beckoned (on 52nd Street)
Artie Shaw and his Orchestra
Helen Forrest, vocalist

At first, Artie Shaw did not even remember having recorded this *Du Barry* confection, and after relistening to his own record, he was pretty sure why. "Strictly speaking, it's not really what I'd call jazz or swing band material," he said in a conversation. "But it's a good example of what the band could do with a tune. If you sing 'Fifty-second Street' in strict tempo it almost sounds like a march; it's a little hard to give it a beat.

"But we obviously worked a bit on this song. In cases like this I'd do the basic sketch, then Jerry Gray—or, later, Lennie Hayton or somebody—would flesh it out and turn it into a full arrangement."

Shaw played the record again. "Listen to that sax section in the first chorus," he said. "You know, if you listen to the Quartet from *Rigoletto*, there's no blend at all. They're all great soloists. But take four guys with medium voices, really train them to breathe and sing properly together, and you get a great blend.

"I mean, there have never been four more dissimilar [saxophone] sounds than Les Robinson, Hank Freeman, Tony Pastor and Georgie Auld, and yet here they sound like a barbershop quartet. Years later, guys like [Henry] Mancini and others told me they'd learned to arrange by listening to records like this one."

Despite the title (and the lyric referring to a band playing swing) there is scant evidence that Cole Porter ever spent much time at the Onyx, the Famous Door, or any of the other 52nd Street haunts. In common with so many of his songs, "When Love Beckoned" is irregularly structured, broken up into sections of 16-16-8-12 bars; its melody, built around a long-noted ascending line, does indeed sound like the trio section of a march. In sum, it is not a tune that might have sprung from the mind of a Stuff Smith, Bunny Berigan, John Kirby, or any of the other regulars on "West Fifty-Two."

Still it is a charming song. And the fact that "Do I Love You?" appeared on the other side of the original Shaw recording indicates that Victor—and Artie—chose their repertoire with the brand-new success of *Du Barry* firmly in mind.

Katie Went to Haiti
Bobby Short

More than a touch of Noël Coward lurks behind the scenes in this ribald tale of virtue compromised by tropic *amour* (in fact, Coward's "In a Bar on the Piccola Marina" covers much of the same ground, its suburban London widow sliding into the temptations of the flesh with little more than token resistance).

How astonishing it seems, in these anything-goes times, that in the world of 1939 even popular songs retained a strictly observed—if largely unspoken—scheme of moral values. Eadie might have been a lady, gold toothpick and all, but the fact that her past was decidedly shady placed her far from the sunny side of the street. By the same token, private secretaries might have weekend flings with Latin lovers in old Havana, but they always returned to the office and good old reality the following Monday.

It was clearly understood that the fallen women of "Moanin' Low" and "My Man" lived with degradation for the sake of love—or at least passion; that the business of "Love for Sale" was not a business for amateurs. But for a respectable (and presumably staunchly middle class) woman to slide avidly into debauchery was rather more serious. Puritanism (defined by the ever-acerbic H. L. Mencken as "the haunting fear that someone, somewhere, may be happy") remained vigilant, ready to express shock and indignation not only that "practically all Haiti had Katie" —but that she had actually enjoyed it!

Ironically enough, one of those who confessed to discomfort and even disapproval at some of Porter's more sexually audacious double entendres was the onetime burlesque-house comic Bert Lahr. "When Cole got dirty it was dirt without subtlety," Lahr said in *Notes on a Cowardly Lion*, assembled by his son John. "Nothing I sang in burlesque was as risque as his lyrics. It would never have been allowed on the burlesque stage."

In the case of the *Du Barry* song "But in the Morning, No," Lahr complained to producer Buddy De Sylva that some of the racier material might drive customers away. De Sylva agreed, decreeing that certain lyrics not be used.

Bobby Short is clearly under no such restrictions here and delivers the full story of Katie's amorous adventures—introduced in the show by Ethel Merman—with precision and obvious élan.

Well, Did You Evah!
Cole Porter and cast of 1956 telecast

This bit of gossipy Porter fun had two incarnations. In *Du Barry* it proved something of a tour de force for twenty-three-year-old Betty Grable. Seventeen years later, as knocked off in *High Society* by Bing Crosby and Frank Sinatra, it was a major hit.

Grable had been around Hollywood since 1930, doing bit parts in movies and singing (and dancing) with dance bands. She had made headlines in 1937 with her marriage to former child star Jackie (the Kid) Coogan. But she had never been on the stage, much less had a starring role.

No wonder producer Buddy De Sylva was a little nervous when his friend, Hollywood agent Louis Shurr, started pitching her for an ingenue role in *Du Barry*. At Shurr's invitation he flew to San Francisco to audition her himself and liked what he heard—and, presumably, saw. He suggested Miss Grable audition directly for Porter.

Shurr set it up—even over her objections that "You know, Louis, I don't sing too well." It is not hard to imagine him, in the familiar accents of the show business agent, firing back, "Lissen, kid, take it from me. When he gets a load of you and that ohh-la-la figure of yours, he's not gonna worry much about the voice."

Which is, in fact, pretty much how things happened. She landed the plummy role of Alice Varton and made the most of "Well, Did You Evah!," sung as a duet with Charles Walters (the same Charles Walters who later directed *High Society*). The song is a natural comic vehicle, lampooning the relentlessly understated way in which society folk deal with bad news:

> Have you heard that poor, dear Blanche
> Got run down by an avalanche?
> Well, did you evah! What a swell party this is . . .

It also seemed a natural choice when, in 1956, Porter wrote the score for *High Society*, a musical reworking of Philip Barry's stage success, *The Philadelphia Story*, teaming Crosby and Sinatra onscreen for the first time.

Crosby also participated in the 6 October 1956 telecast paying tribute to Porter on the occasion of the release of *High Society*. Once again, the old master reworked his own lyrics for a special use—this time to return the thanks of the stars assembled to thank him for a singular and utterly irreplaceable body of music. Supreme sophisticate, bon vivant, snob, dedicated master craftsman, wit, chronicler of an era, observer of human foibles, and so very much more—Cole Porter was one of a kind.

Leave the last word to Irving Berlin. Porter, he said, "was the greatest of us all."

Porter with Louis Armstrong, one of the stars of the 1956 film, High Society, *for which Porter composed the score.*

The Principal Performers

By Richard M. Sudhalter

BERT AMBROSE (1897–1973), who led one of Great Britain's most popular dance orchestras for three decades, was once described by British musician-critic Maurice Burman as "a rare mixture of dignity and buffoonery . . . a shrewd, subtle and sophisticated man . . . independent of spirit, proud yet incapable of being snobbish." The last description is particularly revealing, in that during the 1930s Ambrose was the bandleader of choice for the highest echelons of British society, including royalty.

Following the example of his colleague Fred Elizalde at the Savoy, Ambrose opened at the brand-new Mayfair Hotel in 1927 with a band full of instrumental stars imported from the United States. His immediate success established a popularity that never flagged, and the Ambrose Orchestra became a training school for such leaders-to-be as Ted Heath, Lew Stone, Sid Phillips, and Stanley Black. Other Ambrose alumni included hot trombonist George Chisholm, trumpeters Tommy McQuater and Max Goldberg, and singers Vera Lynn, Anne Shelton, Elsie Carlisle, and Sam Browne. The leader also had good instincts for the popularity of a song. Johnny Green sketched out "Body and Soul" while listening to Ambrose at the Mayfair, and the orchestra wound up performing it so frequently that Green was persuaded to publish it.

THE ANDREWS SISTERS, Maxene (b. 1918), LaVerne (1915–1967), and Patti (b. 1920), were easily the most popular female singing group of the World War II years. They combined a good vocal blend with energy, personality, and a kind of extrovert showmanship ideally suited to radio and movies. Inspired by the immensely popular Boswell Sisters of New Orleans, the Minneapolis-born Andrews Sisters began touring on the coast-to-coast RKO theater circuit in 1931. Their first hit record, a jazz-flavored performance of the Yiddish favorite "Bei mir bist du schön," came seven years later.

While the Andrews Sisters never approached the Boswells for imagination or sheer musicianship, their popularity far outdistanced that of the earlier trio. Industry sources estimate their record sales at over sixty million, including such perennials as "Pistol-Packin' Mama," "South America, Take It Away," "Don't Fence Me In" (all with Bing Crosby), "Rum and Coca-Cola," "Beer Barrel Polka," "Hold Tight," and "I'll Be with You in Apple Blossom Time."

LOUIS ARMSTRONG (1901–1971) is perhaps the most important performer in the history of jazz and one of the pivotal figures of American popular music. Almost singlehandedly he developed, in the 1920s, a majestic trumpet style that transformed jazz from a largely ensemble music into a soloist's art. He also originated and brought to fruition a manner of singing, of phrasing a melodic line, that has had an effect on every area of popular vocalism. As Henry Pleasants put it in *The Great American Popular Singers*, those who heard Armstrong learned to "escape the strictures of the printed notes and the prescribed rhythms, to distort meter in favor of a more flexibly musical prosody, to work out of syllables rather than words, to take the melodic and rhythmic structure of a song apart and put it together again so the singer talked as he sang and sang as he talked."

In a more general sense, jazz critic Leonard Feather wrote that "Americans, unknowingly, live part of every day in the house that Satch built. A riff played by a swinging band on television, a nuance in a Sinatra phrase, the Muzak in the elevator, all owe something to the guidelines that Louis set." Toward the end of the 1930s Armstrong began a gradual transformation from jazz attraction into a more general entertainer, and in so doing became a beloved figure in every corner of the globe.

FRED ASTAIRE (1899–1987) won fame in his lifetime as dancer, singer, actor, and even songwriter. But it is perhaps most appropriate to regard him in the round as one of the century's truly seminal entertainers. Born Frederick Austerlitz in Omaha, Nebraska, he was performing by age five, and while in his teens had a dancing act in vaudeville with his elder sister, Adele. By the beginning of the 1920s they were headliners on Broadway and on the London stage, appearing in *Lady, Be Good* (1924), *Funny Face* (1927), *The Band Wagon* (1931), and other hits of the era.

Adele's marriage to the English Lord Charles Cavendish in 1932 left her brother in a career dilemma, one resolved for him later that year when Cole Porter played "After You,

Who?" for him and won his agreement to appear in *Gay Divorce*. From then on it was just a matter of time and talent. Telling journalist Lucius Beebe that "the stage is beginning to worry me a bit," he set out for Hollywood and found his destiny. After *Dancing Lady*, in which he partnered Joan Crawford in several dance routines, he won a spot in RKO's *Flying Down to Rio* (1933), in which, at the suggestion of producer Lou Brock, he was teamed with a twenty-two-year-old emigrant from Broadway named Ginger Rogers.

The films that followed—*The Gay Divorcée* (1934), *Top Hat* (1935), *Swing Time* (1936), *Shall We Dance* (1937), and the rest—are landmarks of American entertainment. They both embody the fantasy life of depression-era America and transcend it, with Astaire and Rogers virtually redefining the entire notion of popular dance, particularly as applied to the screen. "Fred Astaire," said director Rouben Mamoulian, "makes it look easy only by taking the greatest of pains. He works harder than any newcomer. He never lets up. You'd think his entire life and future depended upon the outcome of each dance. He keeps at the top because he does the impossible—he improves on perfection."

Astaire demonstrated almost equal talent as a singer. Though his baritone voice was thin and a bit reedy, his sense of phrase, unerring intonation, and naturally light rhythmic touch made him a favorite of Irving Berlin, George Gershwin, and other premier songwriters. As singer Sylvia Syms, a lifelong admirer, put it recently, "he danced words." He also swung: in the early 1950s he recorded a three-LP collection of his hits backed by a band of jazz stars including pianist Oscar Peterson and tenor saxophonist Flip Phillips. He was superbly at home.

As a dramatic actor, Astaire excelled in such films as *On the Beach*, in which he nearly stole top honors from the two major stars, Gregory Peck and Ava Gardner. His songwriting efforts include the rhythmically engaging "I'm Building Up to an Awful Letdown" (lyrics by Johnny Mercer), as well as "Just like Taking Candy from a Baby," which he sang and danced on record with Benny Goodman's swing band, and "Life Is Beautiful," which later became the theme song for television's *Tonight Show*.

Perhaps Bing Crosby spoke for all America when he said of Astaire, "There never was a greater perfectionist; there never was, or never will be, a better dancer, and I never knew anybody more kind, more considerate, or so completely a gentleman. I love Fred and I admire and respect him. I guess it's because he's so many things I'd like to be, and am not."

AL BOWLLY (1898–1941) is a throwback to the notion of the medieval troubadour, a wandering poet-musician able to make his way by singing for his supper. Born of a Greek father and Lebanese mother in Lourenco Marques, Mozambique, formerly Portuguese East Africa, Bowlly grew up in Johannesburg and before he was twenty-five had sung in Shanghai, Surabaya, Calcutta, Berlin, and Munich. In 1928 he arrived in London where his emotional manner of singing, allied with his charm and dark good looks, won him a job with Fred Elizalde's Orchestra at the prestigious Savoy Hotel. "Al Bowlly is a real find," proclaimed the *Melody Maker* at the time.

Not long after, Bowlly began singing with other top bands, including those of Lew Stone and, on records, arranger-composer Ray Noble. By the time Noble opened New York's Rainbow Room in 1935, with Bowlly and an all-star American band, Bowlly was one of the most frequently recorded and beloved vocalists in the world.

His singing was direct and passionate, which was no mere posture: "Al was a very sentimental guy who had no trouble showing his emotions," historian George T. Simon has written. Bowlly returned to England when Noble moved to Hollywood and was in the process of building a new solo career when he was killed by a bomb during a Nazi air raid on London.

RUBY BRAFF (b. 1927) seemed, at the outset, the right man at the wrong time. A trumpet stylist of majesty and lyric power, he made his first impact in the 1950s, when fashions in jazz brass playing had traded the emotionalism of Louis Armstrong and Bix Beiderbecke for the anti-romanticism of Dizzy Gillespie and other architects of the bebop movement. But Braff's early records, including an unsurpassed series of duo performances with pianist Ellis Larkins, announced an eloquent new solo voice, lush of tone and fertile of romantic imagination.

Since then, Braff's independent spirit and unwavering dedication to the primacy of melody have seen him through; in later life he has become something of a standard-bearer for a new generation of players who have rediscovered melodic jazz. "Improvisation is adoration of the melody," he told *The New Yorker* jazz critic Whitney Balliett. "It's imagination coupled with a strong sense of composition. The best improvisations I've heard came out of melodic thinking. When I play 'I Got Rhythm,' I play it because I love the melody, and I keep that melody singing along somewhere in my head. Running its chords doesn't interest me." Braff does not exactly improvise *on* songs; rather, as Balliett states it, he "heats them up so that their colors and curves and textures gleam and shine. He points up their treasures, but leaves them intact."

ROSEMARY CLOONEY (b. 1928) found fame and fortune relatively early in her singing career, but at high cost. Ken-

Fred Astaire at the time of Gay Divorce, *his first stage appearance without sister Adele and his last Broadway show.*

tucky-born, she was twenty-three when her recording of the pop novelty "Come on-a My House" hit the top of the charts. With Columbia Records A & R man Mitch Miller calling the shots, she also scored with such novelties as "Botch-a-Me" and "This Ole House," as well as straightforward ballad readings of "Tenderly," "Half as Much," "Hey There," and others. But all this early success led to neurosis, unhappiness and, ultimately, a major breakdown.

In the 1970s, after years of personal and psychological crises, Clooney finally came into her own as a singer of warmth, humor, and great rhythmic flexibility. With the help of her friend and admirer Bing Crosby she returned to performing, appearing with him in his shows in the United States and abroad. In recent years she has continued to appear widely and has recorded a succession of fine albums, usually backed by talented jazz instrumentalists. "Musicians are the greatest people in the world," she wrote in her autobiography *This for Remembrance*. "I have great respect for them, and I think it's mutual. I understand them. I understand their sense of humor because I have very much the same sense of humor."

EMIL COLEMAN (1894–1965) was for five decades the toast of New York high society, one of a small circle of orchestra leaders who supplied the music to which the rich and famous carried on their well-publicized social lives.

Long a fixture at such select Manhattan spots as the Persian Room of the Plaza Hotel and the Sert and Empire rooms at the Waldorf, Emil seemed to have a knack for choosing music appropriate to every occasion, remembering the favorite songs of debutantes and dowagers alike.

Born in Odessa, Russia, one of nine children of a Jewish academician, young Emil grew up in an atmosphere of privilege, far from the anti-Semitic pogroms sweeping his homeland at the turn of the century. He attended Odessa University, but after the abortive revolution of 1905 his father transplanted the children, their nurse, and the family cook to England, settling at Watford, north of London. Through an uncle's benevolence, Coleman enrolled at a local music school, where he graduated with high honors in 1911.

Rather than pursue further studies he went to work as a pianist, on one occasion playing at a beer garden in the rough-and-tumble Earl's Court district with a twenty-piece, all-woman band. In 1912, while working at a Lyons Corner House restaurant and doubling as coach of an opera-in-English company, he met and fell in love with soprano Ruth Zausner; they were married and the next year were off to the United States on a concert tour, Coleman as his new wife's accompanist.

His life from then on was a whirlwind. He appeared under the sponsorship of Sigmund Romberg at Bustanoby's Restaurant, 39th Street and Broadway, and did so well he shortly found himself fronting his own orchestra in a room specially created for him. A visiting Cuban millionaire hired him for a party in Havana, and soon he was leading his own society orchestra there, earning a princely $300 a week.

Back in New York, Coleman became one of the city's top society bandleaders, with long engagements at the best rooms. It was he, apparently, who originated what became a basic convention of society music: the ten-to-fifteen-song medley, for up to half an hour of uninterrupted dancing.

Society clients were devoted to him. In 1947 he estimated that he had played for some five hundred coming-out parties. Coleman orchestras were regular features of cotillions, charity balls, presidential inaugurals, and visits by European royalty. When Jacqueline Kennedy decided to throw a lavish birthday party for her husband at the Waldorf, Coleman was her first choice.

He made his first records in 1919 and recorded regularly thereafter, usually for labels in the Brunswick group. A small, genial, mustachioed man with an eternally perturbed air, Coleman had an ear for good musicianship, often hiring men who later went on to become leaders or star soloists. During the 1950s, in the infancy of television, he had his own weekly television show.

Coleman died of the effects of a stroke on 28 January 1965, three days before he was due to play at an inaugural ball for President Lyndon Johnson. His son, Emil, Jr., fulfilled the commitment, leading the orchestra in his father's stead.

[HARRY LILLIS] "BING" CROSBY (1904–1977) arrived with the microphone and used it to almost singlehandedly revolutionize popular singing. As vocalist with Paul Whiteman's immensely successful orchestra of the late 1920s, he was able to record often, quickly adapting his high baritone to the intimacy afforded by the new electric recording techniques.

Born in Spokane, Washington, Crosby had played drums in his school days and developed a lifelong affection for jazz, one nurtured further by association during his Whiteman days with such jazz immortals as cornetist Bix Beiderbecke, saxophonist Frank Trumbauer, and the brothers Tommy and Jimmy Dorsey.

Crosby's vocal approach was brand-new. In one writer's words, instead of singing *at* people in the manner of Al Jolson and other popular entertainers of the day, he sang *to* them. It was as if he were confiding to the microphone, and therefore to each listener. One early commentator, Charles Henderson, described it as "the feeling that he's letting you in on something very important to you, something he wants to tell you about, now that you and he are alone together."

The 1930s made Crosby a major star, as a combination of radio, records, and movies brought his name, his face, and above all the relaxed sound of his voice into millions of American homes. "Was there really ever a time," musician-producer Larry Carr wrote during the 1960s, "when the familiar, friendly voice of Bing Crosby wasn't a part of our lives and memories?"

Characteristically, Crosby took it all in stride. In his autobiography, *Call Me Lucky*, he clung to his assertion that every man who heard him "believes firmly that he sings as well as I do, especially when he's in the bathroom shower.... It's my hunch that most men feel that if they had gotten the opportunities I've had, they could have done just as well." His point was well made. Crosby *did* sound like the guy next door, and in so doing made popular singing accessible.

The more he matured, the more thoroughly Crosby mastered a delivery based on understatement. His singing seemed conversational, almost casual—yet its effect could be as intense as that produced by far more strident vocal efforts. In the end, the key to his eternal appeal is both simple and mysterious. Henry Pleasants put it well: "As with John McCormack or Richard Tauber or Louis Armstrong, when we hear Bing Crosby we recognize the voice of an old and treasured friend."

BOB CROSBY (b. 1913) found very early in his professional life that being Bing's kid brother could be both advantage and handicap. The name (and a strong facial resemblance) made him easy to spot, but as a singer he could not begin to compete. Perhaps it is fitting, then, that Bob found his show-business destiny elsewhere, leading one of the distinguished bands of the 1930s.

The Bob Crosby Orchestra was an unusual ensemble in that it specialized in big-band (and occasionally small-band) dixieland, highlighted by such outstanding soloists as trumpeters Yank Lawson and Billy Butterfield and New Orleans natives Eddie Miller on tenor saxophone and Ray Bauduc on drums. "It was a band with tremendous spirit," George T. Simon has written, "one filled with men who believed thoroughly in the kind of music they were playing and, what's more, who respected and admired one another as musicians and as people."

Long after his band broke up, Crosby continued to play dance and concert dates and appear on television, fronting groups that included as many of his former sidemen as he could assemble. "I was the only guy in the business who made it without any talent," he was fond of saying in later years. He may have been talking about his singing, but the abiding excellence of the Crosby band bears witness to how wrong, overall, he was.

XAVIER CUGAT (1900–1990) was born with the twentieth century, on New Year's day, and in many respects his career was a uniquely twentieth-century phenomenon. He was a man of many talents, including violinist, bandleader, caricaturist, and raconteur; to borrow the phrase of a later age, he was a natural "media person." Born in Barcelona, Spain, he grew up in Havana, spent part of his youth in Brooklyn, studied in Berlin, and worked as a violinist with various dance bands around New York before organizing his first Latin-flavored ensemble for an engagement at the Cocoanut Grove in Los Angeles.

Cugat's big break came in 1932, when he was asked to front a relief band at New York's Waldorf-Astoria Hotel. His natural showmanship and flair for publicity parlayed this residency into one success after another. In its bright red cutaway jackets, his band looked as good as it sounded, introducing first the rumba, then the conga to American dancers.

In this country Cugat championed quite a few Latin American musicians, including the Mexican composer Alberto Dominguez ("Perfidia," "Frenesi") and the Brazilian Ary Barroso ("Baia," "Brazil"). Offstage, too, he made news. His amorous entanglements with such beauties as Abbe Lane and Charo, both of whom he married, kept the gossip columnists busy. There may have been more authentic Latin bands than Cugat's, but none had a better sense of what the public would love—and what it would long remember.

BILL EVANS (1929–1980) remains, more than a decade after his death, the most universally influential of contemporary jazz pianists. His unique touch, melodic and harmonic imagination, and his conception of a lean, almost ascetic romanticism, have found their way into the work of nearly every keyboard artist working in the jazz world today.

New Jersey–born, Evans made his first solo album in 1956 and seemed—like Jack Teagarden, Lester Young, and a very few others before him—to have arrived mature, fully formed. "His harmonic approach," Brian Priestley has written, "was significant in softening the edges of conventional sequences and pointing the way for pianists to cope with modal jazz." For most of 1958 Evans worked for trumpeter Miles Davis, who paid unaccustomed tribute by remarking that he "plays the piano the way it should be played." Plagued throughout his professional life by drug addiction, Evans died at fifty-one in 1980.

Ella Fitzgerald in the mid-1940s.

ELLA FITZGERALD (b. 1918) has been known throughout most of her long career as "the first lady of song," and there is much accuracy in the sobriquet. Certainly no other singer has brought to the vocal art the consistency of musicianship, clarity, and continuing accessibility that have been her hallmarks. Born in Newport News, Virginia, Ella was orphaned early, came to New York with an aunt and, when barely into her teens, won a Harlem Opera House talent contest by doing an imitation of Connie Boswell. That led to a job with Chick Webb's orchestra, and to almost universal acclaim. She coauthored her first major record hit with Webb, the nonsense song "A-tisket, A-tasket."

Ella's reputation continued to grow, culminating, during the 1950s, with her definitive "songbook" series of albums, spotlighting the work of George Gershwin, Harold Arlen, Cole Porter, Irving Berlin, Jerome Kern, Duke Ellington, and Johnny Mercer.

Though some critics have found her wanting as an interpreter of lyrics, all agree that Ella's excellence and high standard of performance have brought her vocal stylings to an audience wider and more varied than that of any other singer, with the possible exceptions of Frank Sinatra and her friend and sometime collaborator, Louis Armstrong. Hampered in later life by cataracts and other ills, Ella nonetheless carried on singing, strongly and well, into her seventies.

HELEN FORREST (b. 1918) sang for three of the most prominent leaders of the great band years—Artie Shaw, Benny Goodman, and Harry James. To each assignment she brought simple but effective gifts: a bright, controlled voice, an easy manner of phrasing, and a unique way of personalizing a lyric. It was no small accomplishment, since band singers usually only got one chorus, midway in an arrangement, and generally at danceably bright tempos. That Forrest was able to work so effectively within these constraints bears witness to her skill. "Not only was she unable to choose her tempos," Irving Townsend has written, "she was never allowed the luxury of a ritard; yet by singing sometimes slightly behind the driving beat, by giving warm words special emphasis, and by the soaring quality of her voice she managed to float above it all on emotional currents of her own." After some years as a solo performer she withdrew from music entirely, only to return, more polished than ever, in later life. "I have to perform in public or I'd be incomplete," she wrote in her autobiography, *I Had the Craziest Dream*. "I won't sing without an audience—I love an audience."

BUD FREEMAN (1906–1991) came out of Chicago in the 1920s with a vivid personal jazz style on tenor saxophone, one which owed little to the pioneering efforts of Coleman Hawkins. Gutty and driving, yet possessed of a trenchant wit, his playing represented, in one critic's words, a dry sherry to Hawkins's rich old port. Freeman's own compositions, including "The Eel" and "The Sailfish," encapsulate many of the unusual serpentine figures that are characteristic of his style.

Along with cornetist Jimmy McPartland and clarinetist Frank Teschemacher, Freeman was one of a circle of white musicians who, while still at Chicago's suburban Austin High School, evolved the rhythmically exciting way of playing that came to be known as Chicago Jazz. Though he worked memorably and successfully with several big bands during the 1930s (notably those of Tommy Dorsey, Ray Noble, and Benny Goodman), Freeman was always most at home in small groups such as his own Summa Cum Laude Orchestra, which he led in 1939–40, featuring such longtime colleagues as clarinetist Pee Wee Russell, drummer Dave Tough, and trumpeter Max Kaminsky.

In the early 1970s Freeman became a member of the extravagantly named World's Greatest Jazz Band (co-led by trumpeter Yank Lawson and bassist Bob Haggart), with which he recorded and toured widely. At the end of *You Don't Look like a Musician*, one of his three books of memoirs, Freeman sums things up this way: "I have lived all over the world; I've met every walk of life from the poorest to the richest; I've met the most famous people in the world including royalty and the notorious. I can't think of a better life."

JUDY GARLAND (1922–1969) was fond of saying of herself, "I was born at the age of twelve on the Metro-Goldwyn-Mayer lot," and that wry assessment was pretty close to the truth. A child of show business, she experienced little of conventional childhood or adolescence. Her parents, Ethel and Frank Gumm, were a small-time vaudeville couple who showed no reluctance to incorporate their three toddlers into their traveling act.

Soon the kids were the Gumm sisters, winning raves on their own, particularly twelve-year-old Frances. As *Variety* put it in a 1934 review of an appearance at Graumann's Chinese Theater, "Possessing a voice that, without a p.a. system, is audible throughout a house as large as the Chinese, she handles ballads like a veteran, and gets every note and word over with a personality that hits audiences."

It was just a matter of time before a big break came her way, and it happened after an agent won her an audition singing "Zing! Went the Strings of My Heart" for Louis B. Mayer. The MGM founder was impressed, and, with her new name securely in place, she sang "You Made Me Love You" to a photo of Clark Gable in *Broadway Melody of 1938*. A year later Garland became a major star with the huge success of *The Wizard of Oz*. Other films followed, among them *Meet Me in St. Louis*, *The Harvey Girls*, and *A Star Is Born*.

The speed and sheer height of her ascent took its toll. Even in the years of greatest fame and achievement, her private life was a succession of personal crises, including liberal doses of alcohol, pills, weight gain and loss, marital problems, and, ultimately, artistic lapses. But to borrow a phrase, when she was good she was very, very good—perhaps the very best.

"She had the most utterly *natural* vocal production of any singer I have ever heard," wrote Henry Pleasants in *The Great American Popular Singers*. "It was an open-throated, almost birdlike vocal production, clear, pure, resonant, innocent." Her vibrato, which became uncomfortably prominent late in her career, imparted an emotionally throbbing quality to her best work. Her enunciation was clear and precise, able to carry her above even the overarranged hubbub of such production numbers as this set's "I Happen to Like New York."

Yet none of these qualities explains Garland's uncanny ability to reach people emotionally and move them in sometimes profound ways. "I'm nothing but a pair of lungs and a voice box," she once told an interviewer. So simple an explanation hardly accounts for her way, as one colleague put it, of singing "not to your ears but to your tear ducts."

There was an exuberance, a natural radiance, built into the sound she made and the way she used it. Without doubt it was wholly instinctive, quite unconnected to the erratic, insecure, haunted woman she was in private life.

It's that radiance, above all, that lasts. For millions who revered her and revere her still, Garland will always be the young Dorothy of *The Wizard of Oz*, believing implicitly and with eternal innocence in the happiness awaiting us all somewhere "Over the Rainbow."

BENNY GOODMAN (1909–1986) seemed at first an unlikely candidate for immortality as the symbol of an era. Quiet, studious, and shy, he immersed himself in the study and practice of the clarinet as a boy growing up poor in Chicago. By age thirteen he was working professionally and at sixteen joined Ben Pollack's orchestra and headed for New York. He was soon the talk of the music business: a clarinetist of stunning technique, inventiveness, and swing who fused the work of the great New Orleans pioneers—Johnny Dodds, Jimmy Noone, and others—with myriad other influences (including the melodic grace of cornetist Bix Beiderbecke) in a brilliant and compelling style.

During the depression Goodman enjoyed a comfortable career as a studio free-lancer. He might have been content to go on that way if circumstances had not propelled him into leadership of his own band and, in 1935, national success. By 1937 Goodman's was the most popular band in the country. His Carnegie Hall concert in January of the following year created a sensation at a time when jazz was new to such formal settings.

Goodman could be a difficult taskmaster, and his drive for perfection—along with an apparent obliviousness to the feelings of others—taxed the patience of even the most loyal sidemen. "Benny was a terrific leader," pianist Jess Stacy once said, "but if I'd had any spunk I'd probably have thrown the piano at him." In later life he appeared occasionally in front of both large and small bands and pursued an avid interest in classical and chamber music. Even after his death, Goodman's preeminence remains. As Benny Green put it in *The Reluctant Art*, "Goodman stamped upon the instrument he played a conception so irresistible and so absolute that it has conditioned jazz ever since."

BILLIE HOLIDAY (1915–1959) is usually identified as a jazz singer, perhaps even the quintessential jazz singer. Yet she conforms little to the stereotypical images evoked by that label. She never indulged in scat singing and seldom discarded or distorted the words of a song. On the contrary, she was one of the most dramatic and evocative of lyric interpreters. With limited range and vocal equipment, she managed to convey nuances and subtle shades of emotion in songs not thought to have such depth.

The illegitimate child of a teenage marriage, Eleanora Fagan became Billie Holiday by taking her father's surname and the first name of Billie Dove, an actress of the day. She grew up the hard way: she was raped as a youngster and was working as a prostitute when scarcely a teenager. Yet her singing on her first records is full of girlish buoyancy, even innocence. Made with such musicians as Benny Goodman, Teddy Wilson, Buck Clayton, and her special and lifelong kindred spirit, tenor saxophonist Lester Young, these records are miracles of musical interaction. Holiday came to wider public attention in the early 1940s through her performance of the poem-in-song "Strange Fruit," a bitter indictment of lynching in the South. Though she fought a lifelong, and ultimately losing, battle against drug addiction, she left a legacy of deeply moving interpretations and an approach to singing that continues to affect and inspire vocalists everywhere.

LIBBY HOLMAN (1906–1971) had a knack for making headlines, only some of them connected with her achievements on the musical stage. Born Elizabeth Holtzman in Cincinnati, she came to New York to study law, but instead became one of Broadway's brightest stars of the depression years.

From the top: Billie Holiday, circa 1945; Benny Goodman in 1943; Judy Garland in 1954, at the time of A Star Is Born.

Libby Holman, circa 1930.

Lena Horne recording at RCA Studios in the 1950s.

Torch songs were her specialty. In 1929 she sang "Moanin' Low" in *The Little Show* and brought the house down. In *Three's a Crowd* the following year she introduced John Green's "Body and Soul" and put both herself and the song on the map forever. As Howard Dietz—lyricist for "Something to Remember You By," another one of her hits—remembered her, Libby "was game for anything... a frivolous person who appeared in the nude in her dressing room, and therefore, had a lot of visitors."

In 1932 her private life suddenly became public, indistinguishable from the anguished songs she sang. Her husband Zachary Smith "Skipper" Reynolds, heir to the multimillion-dollar R. J. Reynolds tobacco fortune, was shot to death in the bedroom of their North Carolina mansion, with the singer standing by. After a preliminary verdict of suicide, a zealous local lawman persuaded the coroner to reopen the case, and amid garish publicity Libby Holman was indicted for murder.

The Reynolds family then stepped in, got the charges thrown out, and Miss Holman went free. But the mystery of Skipper's death was never solved, and a legal technicality kept her from inheriting any but a fraction of his fortune. Her career after that tapered off sharply. Libby Holman's last Broadway appearance was in Porter's *You Never Know*, in which she sang the title song.

She married again in 1941, this time to the distinguished aviator Ralph Holmes; but the union ended in separation, followed by her husband's suicide in 1945. During those years her professional—and some hinted personal—association with black folksinger Josh White kept her name in the newspapers, particularly the gossip columns.

Tragedy struck Miss Holman again in 1950, when her son Christopher, child of the marriage to Reynolds, was killed while climbing a California mountain. She took refuge in performance, touring the United States and abroad with her one-woman show, "Blues, Ballads and Sin Songs."

Toward the end of her life she married again, this time happily, and recorded an LP, *The Legendary Libby Holman*, on which she reprised "Body and Soul," "Moanin' Low," and various of her other successes.

LENA HORNE (b. 1917) has spent most of her long career triumphing over obstacles that might have daunted a lesser performer. Again and again she fought back against bigotry and racial discrimination, always with a dignity and elegance that has left even her critics gasping.

As Roy Hemming and David Hajdu put it in their *Discovering Great Singers of Classic Pop*, her beauty and bearing "have sometimes tended to overshadow the fact that she is also one of her generation's finest singers, with a sultry, sensual voice of considerable range, flexibility and focused power."

Born Helena Calhoun Horne in Brooklyn, she was a dancer at Harlem's Cotton Club by the time she was sixteen, and a band singer with Noble Sissle and Charlie Barnet before she was much into her twenties. She appeared with Teddy Wilson and drummer Big Sid Catlett at Cafe Society Downtown, then moved quickly through a Carnegie Hall concert, an RCA Victor recording contract, and regular spots on NBC's popular "Chamber Music Society of Lower Basin Street" radio series. She won critical praise for her appearances in two Hollywood films, *Cabin in the Sky* (in which her performance nearly upstaged that of Ethel Waters, one of her idols) and *Stormy Weather*. Her singing of the title song in the latter linked it with her forever in the public mind. "I've had stormy weather all my life," she has said. "If anybody can sing about the trouble I've seen, it's this old broad."

Her MGM debut in *Panama Hattie* in 1942 was typical of Hollywood's handling of her. For the sequence in which she sang "Just One of Those Things" the studio tried to pass her off as a Latin bombshell, complete with Carmen Miranda costume. Hollywood clearly did not know what to do with a dazzling beauty who would not accept the cavalier treatment usually given black performers, and who insisted on a clause in her MGM contract stipulating that she would never have to play maids or prostitutes.

Inevitably, her career ran aground over the matter of her race. Her activism in the Screen Actors' Guild on behalf of black performers angered studio heads, and her biracial 1947 marriage to arranger-conductor Lennie Hayton put an end to Hayton's film career. She lost out on the much-coveted part of the mulatto Julie in the remake of *Show Boat*—the role going, ironically, to her friend Ava Gardner.

The Haytons moved East and ran into trouble even finding a place to live in Manhattan. When the McCarthy witch-hunts of the 1950s began, Lena's name turned up in the infamous *Red Channels*. Work dried up. Yet she persevered, all the while growing as a singer. Her combination of charisma and musicianship prompted the late Elsa Maxwell to declare that "she has put poise into seduction, dignity into daring; she has given glamour manners."

Manners and dignity can exact their price. For many, Lena Horne's name became synonymous with a kind of studied aloofness, leaving her open to accusations of coldness. "The image I chose to give," she has said, "is of a woman the audience can't reach and therefore can't hurt."

All that changed dramatically in 1981 when, a beautiful and svelte sixty-four, she took Broadway by storm with her one-woman show, *A Lady and Her Music*. "Not only have we heard a great singer top what we thought to be her best work," Frank Rich enthused in the *New York Times*, "but we've witnessed an honest-to-God *coup de theatre*."

Her triumph also enabled her to become far more outspoken on racial matters. Moving into her seventies, she

Gertrude Lawrence in 1939.

showed no sign of losing her unique energy, or the sense of charisma that has won generations of admirers. "Let us resign ourselves," author-producer Nat Shapiro once wrote, "to the fact that Lena cannot be easily defined or categorized. We can, however, be properly grateful to the deity of our choice that we are here, on her planet, in her time."

HAL KEMP (1905–1940) led a popular dance band at the University of North Carolina during the 1920s and turned professional after graduation. After beginning as a "hot dance" unit (which included trumpeter Bunny Berigan), Kemp switched musical policies and became, in George T. Simon's phrase, "one of the greatest sweet bands of all time." He caught on with the public through a long stand at Chicago's Blackhawk Restaurant and later at the Madhattan Room of the Hotel Pennsylvania in New York.

The Kemp style was deceptively simple, using smooth, full-voiced ensembles, unison saxophones and clarinets, and clipped phrasing by muted trumpets, all with great attention to dynamics. Another characteristic was the slightly breathless crooning of Skinnay Ennis. With arrangements by pianist John Scott Trotter, Kemp's close friend and collaborator since college days, the band was particularly inspired by show tunes. Its success was cut brutally short on 19 December 1940 when Kemp, en route to an opening in San Francisco, was killed in an auto crash. Ennis, Trotter, and several others tried to keep things going, but ultimately acknowledged that the Hal Kemp Orchestra had passed on with its leader.

TEDDI KING (1929–1977) was a small miracle. Scarcely five feet tall, she was blessed with a voice of great purity and a truly affecting tenderness of delivery. Born in Boston, she came to New York in the mid-1950s after an apprenticeship that included associations with such jazzmen as trumpeter Ruby Braff and pianists George Shearing and Nat Pierce. She attracted attention immediately. One admirer rapturously—if somewhat hyperbolically—described her voice as "both erotic and otherworldly." Before long she had a recording contract with RCA Victor and had made several excellent LPs. There was even a hit record, "Mr. Wonderful," in 1957. Her voice, meanwhile, took on even greater color as her sense of lyric interpretation deepened.

Teddi King seemed to have the world at her feet when, in 1970, she fell ill with Lupus Erythematosus; she lived the rest of her life in pain, as the disease destroyed her body and its ability to resist infection. Yet she sang on, made several outstanding albums, faced her infirmity with courage and good cheer, and died much too soon, struck down when a November cold, misdiagnosed, turned overnight to meningitis.

TEMPO KING (1915–1939) made his first records in 1936 and died suddenly three years later. But his singing on his approximately fifty-five Bluebird and Vocalion recordings is consistently spirited; the band, too, usually features such top jazzmen as the brothers Joe (clarinet) and Marty (cornet) Marsala and guitarist Eddie Condon. Little is now remembered about Tempo King, save that he made his reputation in Florida and that his recordings featured a skilled pianist in the Fats Waller style named Queenie Ada Rubin. She, too, remains an undeservedly obscure figure. An item in *Down Beat* magazine in August 1939 states simply that Tempo King was "stricken while rehearsing a new band, and died in New York June 25 of 'intestinal complications.'" It mentions that he was twenty-four and was survived by his mother, father, and several sisters.

ELLIS LARKINS (b. 1923) is, for fellow musicians as well as for the public, a definition of elegance and taste at the keyboard. Conservatory-trained (at Peabody and Juilliard), he brings to the piano a sound and touch, a sense of balance and restraint, that long made him a favorite in such choice New York settings as Cafe Society, the Blue Angel, and more recently, Michael's Pub, the Cookery, and the Carnegie Tavern.

Born in Baltimore, Larkins worked with clarinetist Edmond Hall in the 1940s and during the following decade accompanied performers as disparate as harmonica virtuoso Larry Adler and vocalist Joe Williams. He is perhaps best known for a series of duo recordings made in the 1950s with trumpeter Ruby Braff, which achieved a rapport and unanimity of musical purpose rare even in jazz. Singer Anita Ellis provided insight into Larkins in a conversation with Whitney Balliett: "He listens and invents," she said. "He composes all the time. And he doesn't compromise. He plays and you have to *sing*. . . . Ellis is never dégagé. . . I sometimes think of Ellis's playing as being so of a piece that it comes down to one note—a perfect, hypnotic note."

GERTRUDE LAWRENCE (1898–1952) was a true lady of the theater, who radiated as much charm and downright charisma offstage as on. Though not possessed of a strong singing voice, she had a unique presence, an ability to project, that captivated audiences on both sides of the Atlantic.

Gertrude Alexandr[i]a Dagmar Lawrence-Klasen was born in London to a show-business couple who apparently thought nothing of leaving her in a clothes basket in their dressing room during performances. By age four she was hawking their programs in the lobbies of music halls and at ten was onstage, dancing in the popular pantomime, *Babes in the Wood*. Her lifelong friend Noël Coward, who met her in these early years, remembered her as "a vivacious child with ringlets to whom I took an instant fancy."

After seven years touring in the English provinces, she landed in London as understudy to up-and-coming Beatrice Lillie—and, in classic show-business fashion, went on for her one night and became a star.

It was as a joint lead with Lillie that Miss Lawrence made her American debut in *Andre Charlot's Revue of 1924*, singing "Limehouse Blues." Her performance of the song, with its haunting theme of white slavery in the back alleys of London's East End, made her a sensation on this side of the Atlantic.

After that her career simply took off. She was in the Gershwins' *Oh, Kay!* (1926); *The International Revue* (1930); *Private Lives* (1931), opposite Coward in a part he wrote expressly for her; and, in 1933, Porter's *Nymph Errant*. In 1935 she toured the United States as Susan in Rachel Crothers's *Susan and God* and broke attendance records everywhere.

London and New York audiences, dazzled by her range and emotional depth, took to her with equal fervor in Coward's *Tonight at 8:30* (1936), a series of nine short plays performed three per night. Other Lawrence triumphs included *Skylark* (1939), *Lady in the Dark* (1941)—for which one critic lauded her as "the greatest feminine performer in the theater"—and a 1946 revival of Shaw's *Pygmalion*. Though her film career had begun in England during the 1920s, she did not head for Hollywood until 1950, when she appeared as Amanda in *The Glass Menagerie* alongside Kirk Douglas and Jane Wyman.

Offstage, Miss Lawrence was equally esteemed as a founder and first vice president of the American Theater Wing. During World War II she was a colonel in the U.S. Ambulance Corps and a lieutenant in the Red Cross Motor Corps.

Her last, and perhaps best-known, role was that of Anna Leonowens, the kindly English governess in *The King and I*, opposite Yul Brynner. It was while playing that part that the leukemia she had fought so valiantly over many months finally killed her. She was only fifty-four.

BARBARA LEA (b. 1929) can lay easy claim to being among the most intelligent of all singers, in both the musical and intellectual senses of the word. Her understanding of the levels of meaning in a lyric is enviable: she clearly thinks long and well about a song before ever attempting to sing it, and that emerges in her performances. Her intelligence is also musical, reflected in her phrasing, rhythmic placement, and use of vocal resonances.

Born in Detroit, she took a music major at Wellesley and while there involved herself in Boston's traditional jazz circles. Her affinity for this style remains to this day in her choice of accompanists and associates. She is an astute observer of music and musicians, expressing her views clearly and often forcefully. "There are many singers who *use* music," she told an interviewer. "I resent that. Music is sacred. The song has to control the performance. Doing anything else—employing this or that trick—to make the audience applaud is an outrage. Then you are making them applaud *you*."

Lea is also a founder-member, along with singer-pianist DARYL SHERMAN (b. 1949), of MISTER TRAM ASSOCIATES, a quartet of musical friends who began performing as a group some years ago after long individual associations. Miss Sherman, Rex Reed has written, "sings in an uncluttered, straightforward manner that illuminates every nuance of a song without masquerade. The way she turns Cole Porter's 'Dream Dancing' into a slow, sleepwalking ballad of celestial delight indicates that in a saner age she could even have made hit records."

MARY MARTIN (1913–1990) launched her Broadway career in 1938 singing "My Heart Belongs to Daddy" in *Leave It to Me* and half a century later was still singing it. Was it really true that the little girl from Texas had no idea what the words meant until old pro Sophie Tucker, also in the cast, clued her in?

She never told. But what is certain is that the show's success led to a movie contract with Paramount, and directly to a charming guy named Richard Halliday, who became—in no particular order—her producer, professional adviser, and beloved husband.

She did well enough in films, particularly *Birth of the Blues*, in which she teamed with Bing Crosby and jazz trombone great Jack Teagarden in singing "The Waiter and the Porter and the Upstairs Maid." Back in New York, she starred in the Kurt Weill–Ogden Nash *One Touch of Venus*, where she sang the haunting "Speak Low."

Mary Martin hit the top in 1949, with the role of the "cockeyed optimist," Ensign Nellie Forbush, in Rodgers and Hammerstein's *South Pacific*. For one thousand performances, the pint-size Texan brought audiences to their feet with "I'm Gonna Wash That Man Right Outta My Hair," "A Wonderful Guy," and the rest, playing opposite onetime Metropolitan Opera basso Ezio Pinza.

Next came Peter Pan, a role she said she had always wanted to play. Neverland, she wrote in her autobiography, *My Heart Belongs*, "is the way I would like real life to be: timeless, free, mischievous, filled with gaiety, tenderness and magic."

Born in Weatherford, Texas, to a lawyer and a violin teacher, Mary Martin grew up singing. At five she was piping "When Apples Grow on Lilac Trees" at a fireman's ball and

Mary Martin in 1941.

Barbara Lea.

not long into her teens was singing on a local radio station. Her marriage at sixteen to an accountant named Benjamin Hagman produced a son, who as the actor Larry Hagman went on to become the infamous J. R. Ewing of television's long-running *Dallas* series.

After *Peter Pan* came her starring role of Maria von Trapp in Rodgers and Hammerstein's last collaboration, *The Sound of Music*. "She's an extraordinary trouper," Rodgers wrote in his autobiography, *Musical Stages*. "In all the years I've known her, I have never seen her give a performance that was anything less than the best that was in her."

She won new admirers in 1966 by playing (and singing) opposite Robert Preston in the demanding two-actor virtuoso piece *I Do, I Do*, which traced the development of a marriage over several decades.

Mary Martin was a star. Even in laid-back Weatherford they commemorated her success with a sign on the courthouse lawn: "Weatherford, Texas, home of watermelons and Mary Martin." Her suitably phlegmatic reaction: "I never got top billing in my home town."

All who knew and worked with Miss Martin have spoken with awe of her inner warmth and her seemingly boundless enthusiasm for life. "More than any of her peers," Mel Gussow wrote in her *New York Times* obituary, "she was what she played, and she incarnated the songs that she sang." In fact, he went on, it would not be far wrong to regard her as "the heyday of the Broadway Musical."

TONY MARTIN (b. 1912) began his musical career during the 1930s as Al Morris, a saxophonist in various West Coast dance bands, including that of Tom Gerun, in which he sat alongside a young Woody Herman. Blessed with matinee idol good looks, Morris tried to break into movies, landing a bit part in the Fred Astaire–Ginger Rogers film *Follow the Fleet*. A year later he was in *Sing, Baby, Sing* and married its star, Alice Faye. By now known as Tony Martin, he got a singing shot on George Burns and Gracie Allen's radio show, began making records, and even won a few larger movie roles.

Martin's vocal was an outstanding feature of Ray Noble's popular 1938 recording of his own "I Hadn't Anyone Till You," which opened the way to more record successes, including several songs derived from classical or foreign themes: "Tonight We Love" (Chopin), "I Get Ideas" (the Argentinian pop song "Adios Muchachos"), "Kiss of Fire" (the tango "El Choclo"), and "Stranger in Paradise" (Borodin). Martin is married to dancer and movie/theater star Cyd Charisse.

JOHNNY MERCER (1909–1976) was unique among the great lyricists—a folk poet whose sensibility embraced both the sophistication of modern urban life and the simple, abiding truths of small-town America. Born in Savannah, Georgia, he made his first national impact in the early 1930s, singing (sometimes scat-singing) with Paul Whiteman's large orchestra and dashing off occasional songs with such partners as Hoagy Carmichael and Whiteman violinist-songwriter Matty Malneck.

By 1934 he was writing for movies, showing a particular flair for lyrics that evoked strong images of home and hearth, simple pleasures that touched listeners at all levels of society. His "Jamboree Jones" of 1936, for example, tells the unlikely story of a studious clarinet player who becomes a football hero just by swinging out at a crucial game and inspiring the team to victory. In common with many other Mercer classics ("I'm an Old Cowhand," "Dream," "You Must Have Been a Beautiful Baby," "The Days of Wine and Roses," "Skylark"), it suggests a world far from that of George Gershwin, Jerome Kern, and, indeed, Cole Porter.

Yet it is typical of his artistry that he was able to collaborate successfully with composers as varied as Walter Donaldson, Richard Whiting, Harry Warren, Duke Ellington, Rube Bloom, Harold Arlen, and Kern himself. Mercer's world was one characterized, in the words of his biographer Bob Bach, by "a native humor, a keen insight into the nation's speech habits, and an originality of thought as refreshing as the scent of magnolias."

He brought that originality to each song, including such sophisticated efforts as "Laura" and "When the World Was Young," as well as "I'm Old Fashioned" and "You Were Never Lovelier," both with Kern. In the early 1940s Mercer teamed with fellow lyricist B. G. (Buddy) De Sylva and businessman Glenn Wallachs to start Capitol Records. He also remained active as one of the most engaging of singers, often teaming up with old friends Louis Armstrong, Jack Teagarden, Bing Crosby, and Judy Garland.

MABEL MERCER (1900–1984) possessed a precious and singular art: the ability to find the core of a song and make it intensely personal for every listener. That required a blend of musical and dramatic skills, to make each song into a small world instantly accessible to all.

Born in the north of England to a vaudeville couple, Mercer spent her girlhood on the road as part of the family song-and-dance act. By the 1930s she had gravitated to Paris, where she soon became part of the glamorous circle at the left bank club run by her friend Ada "Bricktop" Smith.

"Bricktop's was very chic, and money was plentiful," she told Whitney Balliett. "Sometimes we'd sing all night, and once I remember stopping in a cafe on the way home and listening to Louis Armstrong and Django Reinhardt, the Gypsy guitarist, playing duets together. They were still there at noon, playing, just the two of them."

Tony Martin, of "Begin the Beguine" fame.

Mabel Mercer.

Ethel Merman in 1936, the year she starred in Red, Hot and Blue!

She came to the United States in 1938 and began a career singing in the best of Manhattan's supper clubs, among them the Ruban Bleu, Tony's, and the Byline Room. As she went from strength to strength, her reputation grew among her fellow performers. They came to listen—and went away Mercer devotees.

Critic-essayist George Frazier, never profligate where praise was concerned, rhapsodized over "her marvelous austerity, her matchless enunciation, her empathy for the meaningfulness of a worthwhile lyric." Frank Sinatra listened and learned. A young Margaret Whiting, in New York for the first time, remembered "a very dignified woman who sat in a chair, moved not a muscle, opened her mouth, and spun enchantment. She was economical in everything she phrased, and her phrasing was effortless and graceful."

As the years eroded her vocal capacities, Mercer instinctively found new expressive means. She often appeared to be half singing, half talking a song. Alec Wilder, entranced, called it her "graceful parlando." It carried her well into her eighties, when she was still able to hold an audience in thrall with a phrase, enunciation of a key word, or even some small expressive gesture.

Balliett, writing about her for *The New Yorker*, extolled her "queenly aura," a blend of grace and composure as she worked her small miracles of interpretation. "I think constantly about the lyrics and what they mean," she told him. "I try and make my listeners feel the vision of what the words are saying."

With characteristic clarity and candor Mercer summed up the essence of her own art. "All of us know about sorrow and tears and laughter," she said, "so it's not my job to sing *my* emotions but to sing my *listeners'* emotions. Then they can take them home with them."

ETHEL MERMAN (1908–1984) burst like a rocket on the 1930 entertainment scene with her show-stopping "I Got Rhythm" in the Gershwin musical *Girl Crazy*. She was anything but a newcomer. She had been singing in theaters and clubs around town since high school, all the while working days as a stenographer. It was at Little Russia, a club on 57th Street and Sixth Avenue, that a theatrical agent named Lou Irwin heard her, liked what he heard, and arranged for her to do a musical short at Warner Brothers. The short is long forgotten, but it set her on her way.

Girl Crazy was her big break. It established the former Ethel Zimmermann in the minds of Broadway theatergoers—and Broadway creators—as a star. Hers was a special chemistry, one that did not always have to do with vocal finesse. As Merman put it in her first autobiography, *Who Could Ask for Anything More?*, "I just stand up and holler and hope that my voice holds out."

Henry Pleasants, writing in *The Great American Popular Singers*, got down to specifics: "The vocal sound, by all traditional and conventional criteria, was godawful. When she was belting, which was most of the time, it was raucous, strident, abrasive, brassy, nasal, open and just plain loud." But, he went on, "it was unmistakably, unforgettably hers."

And it inspired Cole Porter, as it had inspired the Gershwins, to create roles and individual songs tailored to her and her "godawful" voice. As she said of herself, "I do one basic thing. I project." And that, above all, is what so many songwriters liked.

Words, music—phrase for phrase, she belted them over the footlights just as they had been written. "I leave the songs the way they come out of the composer's head," she said once. "If it's a good head they'll be good songs without my editing them."

Merman starred in fourteen Broadway shows, including such all-time hits as Irving Berlin's *Annie Get Your Gun* (1946), *Call Me Madam* (1950), and, unforgettably, Jule Styne and Stephen Sondheim's *Gypsy* (1959). Her collaboration with Cole Porter began with *Anything Goes* in 1934, carrying on through *Red, Hot and Blue!* (1936), *Du Barry Was a Lady* (1939), *Panama Hattie* (1940), and *Something for the Boys* (1943).

She was through and through, as several historians have written, a woman of the Broadway theater, at her best on stage. She was less effective on records and radio, and it may be significant that several of the roles she created on Broadway went to others when the plays became movies.

"I don't bother about style," she told an interviewer. "But I do bother about making people understand the lyrics I sing. I honestly don't think there's anyone in the business who can top me at that." Irving Berlin concurred. In fact, it was he who summed up Merman's eternal appeal best when, in counseling other songwriters, he advised, "If you're writing for Merman, be sure your lyrics are good, because they'll be heard."

MISTER TRAM ASSOCIATES. See Barbara Lea.

JOAN MORRIS (b. 1943) and WILLIAM BOLCOM (b. 1938) have carved a unique place for themselves as interpreters of American popular songs. Touring and recording together since the early 1970s, they stress composer accuracy and keep performer stylization to a minimum in approaching the works of Porter, Rodgers and Hart, Berlin, the Gershwins, and others.

Enhanced by Bolcom's rich, full-fingered piano accompaniments, Morris also applies her light mezzo-soprano to a range of material from Stephen Foster to Leiber and Stoller, all with care, clarity, and sensitivity to textual nuance.

A native of Portland, Oregon, Morris is a graduate of Gonzaga University in Spokane, Washington. She studied acting at the American Academy of Dramatic Arts in New York and began concertizing with Bolcom, now her husband, in 1972. They have made over fifteen recordings together and appear in both concert and cabaret settings. Both are on the music faculty at the University of Michigan at Ann Arbor, where Bolcom was made a full professor in 1983.

Equally respected as composer and pianist, Bolcom won the Pulitzer Prize for music in 1988 for his *Twelve New Etudes for Piano*. His penchant for incorporating American popular styles into a contemporary classical framework has helped win him an auspicious and ongoing list of commissions, including those from major orchestras (New York and Philadelphia) and opera companies.

His wife figures prominently in the premieres of virtually all of his vocal works, from *Songs of Innocence and Experience* (text by William Blake) to his cabaret songs to the stage piece *Casino Paradise*; the segment of his Fourth Symphony that uses voice has been carefully orchestrated to complement her small but precise sound.

JESSYE NORMAN (b. 1945) ranks high among the current elite of opera superstars. Capable of vivid emotional projection and gifted with an unusually large range (from a low G to a high C sharp), the stately soprano made her stage debut in 1969 singing the role of Elisabeth in Wagner's *Tannhaüser* at the Deutsche Oper, Berlin.

In common with many other American opera singers, Norman did most of her career apprenticeship in Europe; she made her American operatic debut in 1982, singing Jocasta in Stravinsky's *Oedipus Rex* and Dido in Purcell's *Dido and Aeneas* in a double bill at the Opera Company of Philadelphia. The following year she sang at the Metropolitan Opera for the first time, opening the company's one hundredth-anniversary season as the prophetess Cassandra in Berlioz's *Les Troyens*.

Born in Augusta, Georgia, Norman studied at Howard University, the Peabody Conservatory, and the University of Michigan. Notes *Opera News* editor Patrick J. Smith in *The New Grove Dictionary of American Music*: "Norman's commanding stature and stage presence have made her a major operatic personality.... Her opulent and dark-hued soprano ... at its finest reveals uncommon refinement of nuance and dynamic variety."

Her appearances in recitals and in such televised events as the widely praised 1990 spirituals concert at Carnegie Hall with soprano Kathleen Battle have won her many admirers among a segment of the public that has seldom, if ever, attended opera.

Norman has a vast concert and opera discography. Her interpretation of Porter's "In the Still of the Night" is taken from her first foray into the pop repertoire, a collaboration with John Williams and the Boston Pops entitled *With a Song in My Heart*.

CASPER REARDON (1907–1941) was a prodigy, a prize student of the great harpist Carlos Salzedo. A successful concert career could have been his for the asking, but instead he elected to bridge the wide gulf that, in the 1930s, separated classical music and jazz. Ultimately, he achieved great success in both.

Born in upstate New York, Reardon began harp studies at age nine and soon was a regular attraction on radio station WGY in nearby Schenectady. After two years studying with Salzedo he won a scholarship to the Curtis Institute of Music in Philadelphia, and within a few years had played with both the Cincinnati Symphony and New York Philharmonic.

In 1931, during his Cincinnati sojourn, he doubled on station WLW, famed for its promotion of new talent, playing popular favorites and some jazz. Though admired by colleagues on both sides of the musical fence, he appeared to recognize that his duality of outlook could be professionally risky; as a result, Reardon the jazz harpist was billed on the radio as "Arpeggio Glissandi."

He came to New York and soon found himself in demand as a free-lance artist for radio and recordings. He appeared as soloist with the Casa Loma Orchestra and with the bands of Paul Whiteman and Abe Lyman. When Whiteman's "Three T's"—Jack and Charlie Teagarden and C-melody saxophonist Frank Trumbauer—did a widely publicized club engagement at New York's Hickory House in 1936, Reardon was in the unusual rhythm section. He went to Hollywood to appear in a film and played regularly at clubs in New York and Chicago.

On such recordings as the 1934 "Junk Man" with Jack Teagarden, Reardon's playing is remarkable for the seeming ease with which he adapts the harp to the rhythmic needs of jazz. In this regard he clearly paved the way for such later jazz harpists as Adele Girard and Dorothy Ashby.

Perhaps because he had a foot planted squarely in each camp, Reardon took a singularly ecumenical view of his musical activities. "His big ambition," said a 1937 article in *Metronome* magazine, "is to do in a performing way what Gershwin did in a composing way—i.e. to educate the general long-haired public on the finer points of shorter-haired jazz and actually to elucidate via concerts at Carnegie Hall."

Friends remember Reardon as both a masterful musician and a quiet and deeply courteous man. "He was a consummate musician, that guy," said Bonnie Lake, a respected singer-songwriter and arranger. "There was a gentleness to him, a sweetness. A relaxed air. And everything he played, he played with great skill."

Beginning in 1936, Reardon recorded occasionally under his own name, usually harp solos accompanied by small ensembles playing what appear to be his own imaginative and tightly knit arrangements. He also recorded a musically ambitious suite by Dana Suesse, in a trio setting with the composer and percussionist Chauncey Morehouse.

Reardon was at the height of his musical success when he died suddenly in 1941 of the effects of a liver ailment. He was only thirty-four.

ARTIE SHAW (b. 1910) rose to national popularity during the 1930s as clarinet-playing leader of one of the nation's top swing bands. More than a half-century of comparisons to his rival and fellow clarinetist Benny Goodman have done neither man justice. As a musician and as a personality, Shaw is unique, a thoughtful and articulate man dedicated to a sometimes fiercely stated musical philosophy. It emerged strongly when he put together his first band in 1937. He sought, he has written, "a crystal-clear transparency," enabling the listener to "hear every instrument . . . see all the way through the surface of the music right down to the bottom, as when you look into a clear pool of water and see the sand at the very bottom of the pool."

Shaw's skills as a clarinetist, honed through years as a radio and recording-studio free-lancer, emerged in front of his own band. Gunther Schuller hailed him in *The Swing Era* as "a real master of the clarinet, virtually incomparable in the beauty of his tone and unique in his flawless control of the instrument's highest register." At his best, said Schuller, Shaw was "an uncompromising searcher for the lofty and expressive, for real musical substance." Shaw retired from playing in the 1950s, returning briefly in the 1980s to oversee a new Artie Shaw orchestra led by Boston clarinetist Dick Johnson.

BOBBY SHORT (b. 1926), who has been referred to as "a walking Smithsonian of the golden age of American Popular Song," has done more than any other single performer to keep the works of the great songwriters before the public.

But that is hardly the whole story. Born in Danville, Illinois, the ninth of ten children, he left home at age eleven to seek his fortune as a singer. "I became," he said in his autobiography, *Black and White Baby*, "the colored counterpart of [boy soprano] Bobby Breen." Not for long. As he grew, young Short fell under the influence of such older stars as Fats Waller, Nat Cole, Art Tatum, and Duke Ellington's great singer Ivie Anderson.

By the 1950s Short had established himself as an urbane and charismatic singer and pianist, quite at home in the rarified atmosphere of Manhattan cafe society. His ability to project, both onstage and off, often makes him seem far more imposing than his slight, five-foot, nine-inch frame would suggest. In the words of *The New Yorker*'s Whitney Balliett, "He is a faultless and inventive dresser . . . has a warm, princely bearing, and he has a stunning smile. The resulting impression, as one meets him, is of a tall, poised, and irresistibly attractive man."

But it took a highly successful recording of a 1968 Town Hall concert with Mabel Mercer to put Short on the map. Three years later he began a series of songwriter tributes on record, that to Cole Porter being among the most noteworthy.

Since 1968 Short has been a fixture at the Cafe Carlyle, gathering point and spiritual home for those who seem to yearn for an older, more elegant Manhattan. "I think the Carlyle is one of the last places in the world where you can drink tea with your pinkie out," he told Balliett. "It attracts royalty."

It is to that royalty, many might argue, that Short belongs. "People say that graciousness is finished," he said. "But it isn't. My people respect graciousness. They are ready to be gracious and they respond to graciousness."

CESARE SIEPI (b. 1923) achieved his fame on the opera stage, bringing to every role an uncompromising standard of excellence and freshness. "I have never once sung a performance to be ashamed of," he told an interviewer.

Legions of admirers agree. Sir Rudolf Bing, former manager of the Metropolitan Opera, used to refer to him as "the only [Don] Giovanni in the world," for his portrayal of Mozart's notorious philanderer. He also won widespread praise for his Figaro in another great Mozart opera and for his Mephistopheles in Gounod's *Faust*.

The dashing, six-foot, two-inch basso from Milan was eighteen when he made his professional debut in 1941 at Schio, just outside Venice. Two years later he narrowly escaped the Nazi occupation of Milan, finding refuge in a Swiss detention camp, where he teamed up with his Milanese friend tenor Giuseppe di Stefano in a remarkable series of concerts. In 1945 he sang in the benefit performance to rebuild the opera house at La Scala and five years later made his Metropolitan Opera debut, singing King Philip II of Spain in Verdi's *Don Carlos*. He remained on the Met roster through 1973.

Siepi explains the length and consistency of his career with characteristic practicality: "The way to do it is to choose carefully what you sing, learn it thoroughly, and give the voice plenty of rest between performances."

His Mediterranean charm, good looks, and sumptuous bass timbre brought frequent comparisons to Ezio Pinza. But his Broadway career was far more modest than his colleague's, confined to the short-lived 1962 musical *Bravo Giovanni*. Siepi did guest frequently on "The Voice of

Firestone" and "The Ed Sullivan Show." He was still singing in major opera houses as recently as the mid-1980s.

JAMES STEWART (b. 1908) may be the last of Hollywood's larger-than-life actors, an honor roll that has included Spencer Tracy, Gary Cooper, Clark Gable, Cary Grant, John Wayne, and Stewart's longtime friend, Henry Fonda. His career, spanning more than five decades, numbers close to one hundred pictures.

Stewart was three years out of Princeton when, in 1935, he signed a three-year contract with MGM and made his screen debut in *The Murder Man*, lying in the trunk of a car. After that came success: *You Can't Take It with You* (1938), *Mr. Smith Goes to Washington* (1939), *The Philadelphia Story* (1940), *It's a Wonderful Life* (1946), and three Alfred Hitchcock classics—*Rear Window* (1954), *The Man Who Knew Too Much* (1956), and *Vertigo* (1958).

Despite the range of roles he has played, his calm demeanor and distinctive drawl have remained his widely admired and imitated trademarks. A *New York Times* article once lauded him as a "great behavioral actor"; no doubt the writer was responding, as have millions before and since, to Stewart's ingratiating "aw, shucks" manner.

Born in the town of Indiana, Pennsylvania, James Maitland Stewart caught Hollywood fever as a teenager when his father, who owned the local hardware store, got him a job running the projector at the town's movie theater. At Princeton, he studied architecture and, with his pal Hank Fonda, formed the University Players.

Drafted a year before Pearl Harbor, he saw service during World War II as a member of an Eighth Air Force bomber squad. He returned to Hollywood in 1945 a full colonel, winner of the Air Medal, the Distinguished Flying Cross, the Croix de Guerre, and seven battle stars; in 1959 he was named a brigadier general.

Among Stewart's many honors are an Oscar for *The Philadelphia Story*, a New York Film Critics' Award for *Mr. Smith Goes to Washington*, and the Venice Film Festival Award for *Anatomy of a Murder* (1959).

Besides those already listed, many of Stewart's roles have become American classics. He has played a baseball star (*The Stratton Story*-1949), numerous western heroes (*Winchester 73*, *Broken Arrow*-1950, and *The Man Who Shot Liberty Valance*-1962), romantic leads (*No Highway in the Sky*-1952), aviator Charles A. Lindbergh (*The Spirit of St. Louis*-1957), a bandleader (*The Glenn Miller Story*-1954), an Air Force officer (*Strategic Air Command*-1955), and a number of comic leads (*Harvey*-1950 and *Bell, Book and Candle*-1958), among many others.

In later life Stewart's voice became familiar to a brand-new generation of television viewers with a series of successful commercials for a major soup company.

SYLVIA SYMS (b. 1919) learned her craft the hard—and perhaps ideal—way: by hanging around the musicians she most admired and absorbing the best of what she heard. That meant almost constant attendance, as an utterly fearless teenager, at the bars and jazz joints of 52nd Street; no one, she said, ever bothered her. "Who," she asked an interviewer, "wanted to make passes at a fat Jewish girl from Brooklyn?" These visits brought her early association with such giants as saxophonist Benny Carter, who hired her briefly in the 1940s; pianist Art Tatum, who nicknamed her "Moonbeam Moscowitz"; and Billie Holiday, with whom she cemented a friendship that lasted until the older singer's death in 1959.

Her jazz training, allied to considerable theatrical skills, has made Syms in later life a singer of formidable interpretive power, able to lead a listener into the innermost life of a song. In this connection she is often compared to her longtime friend, Frank Sinatra. Though she had a hit record during the 1950s with "I Could Have Danced All Night," Syms has never become as widely known as her talents might suggest—something she accepts with what Whitney Balliett has termed "a brave and judicious narcissism."

"The only person I have to satisfy now as far as my singing is concerned," she has said, "is me." What is more important to her has been the songs themselves and her relationship to each. "Singing for me is my total cleansing. I have to have a personal, almost physical relationship to the songs I sing."

ART TATUM (1910–1956) was, in the words of trumpeter Roy Eldridge, "probably the last man left who had no trouble finding a place to play after hours." The phrase is revealing, both in its evocation of a pianist able to play for hours and never tire of the wonders he could unearth, and in what it says about Tatum's stature among his fellow musicians. This Toledo-born pianist, nearly blind since childhood, possessed a technique, imagination, and swing that placed him in a class by himself, even in a pianistic world inhabited by the likes of Fats Waller, Teddy Wilson, and Earl "Fatha" Hines.

Cornetist Rex Stewart used to tell of one night when Waller was appearing at Chicago's Sherman Hotel; Waller was playing his own "Honeysuckle Rose" when Tatum walked in. "Suddenly Fats jumped up like he'd been stung by a bee and . . . announced in stentorian tones: 'Ladies and gentlemen, God is in the house tonight. May I introduce the one and only Art Tatum.'" True or apocryphal, the story illustrates the point.

Tatum conquered New York in the early 1930s, first as accompanist for singer Adelaide Hall, later as a solo pianist, and, from 1943, as the leader of an outstanding trio. Though some have objected to his overdecorative approach to improvisation, the more adventuresome qualities of Tatum's play-

From the top: Sylvia Syms, Julie Wilson, and Jessye Norman.

ing are still captivating listeners and fellow musicians long after his death. Part of it, said Tatum trio guitarist Everett Barksdale, was that "he leaves you with a sense of futility.... What you've studied maybe years to perfect he seems able to perform with such ease . . . no apparent effort at all."

ETHEL WATERS (1896–1977) triumphed in later life as a dramatic actress, notably in Carson McCullers's play, *The Member of the Wedding*. Those who know and revere her chiefly for her work on the stage and in films are invariably surprised to learn that Waters also was, in the 1920s and 1930s, a pace-setting and highly influential singer.

From beginnings in black vaudeville (where she was often billed as "Sweet Mama Stringbean" and sang the blues), she emerged in the mid-1920s as a vocalist able to fuse the black and white idioms of the day into a new and compelling way of dealing with popular song material. Her recordings of, among other standards, "Dinah" (which she introduced), "Memories of You," and "Am I Blue?" deeply influenced succeeding generations of singers, including such major figures as Lee Wiley, Ivie Anderson, Mildred Bailey, Billie Holiday, Ella Fitzgerald, and many others.

In Henry Pleasants's words, she was "a transitional figure, and a towering one, summing up all that had been accumulated stylistically from minstrel show, ragtime and coon song, and anticipating the artful, jazz-touched Afro-American inflections of the swing era. . . . She made it all sound so natural and easy and inevitable that the listener was unaware of any physical or intellectual accomplishment, or of the mastering of any special difficulties."

Primarily, however, Waters achieved her greatest triumphs on the musical stage. Irving Berlin, hearing her sing "Stormy Weather" at the Cotton Club, was so moved that he cast her in his 1933 *As Thousands Cheer* on Broadway, alongside Clifton Webb, Helen Broderick, and other stars of the time. Her reading of Berlin's poignant "Suppertime," describing the effects of a lynching on a black family, remains a landmark.

She played her first major dramatic, nonmusical role on Broadway in 1939, appearing as Hagar in *Mamba's Daughters*; she subsequently reaffirmed her supremacy as a singer and musical actress in 1940 in *Cabin in the Sky* (where she made a classic of "Taking a Chance on Love"). She hit her peak in 1950 with *The Member of the Wedding*, first on the stage, then the screen.

She insisted all her life that she did not enjoy singing. "I do it for a living," she told an interviewer, "but I'd rather act." All the same, it is as much for her vocal pioneering as for her acting that Waters is remembered and venerated today. As Pleasants put it, "along with Bessie Smith and Louis Armstrong, she was a fountainhead of all that is finest and most distinctive in American popular singing."

ELISABETH WELCH (b. 1908) found stardom as a "one-song singer"—a performer dropped into a show to do only a single song and bring down the house with it. In 1923 she stepped out of the chorus of *Runnin' Wild* to sing "Charleston" and both stopped the show and helped launch the era's major dance craze. In 1931 she was brought into Cole Porter's *The New Yorkers* to sing "Love for Sale" and stole top honors. It was the same story in London two years later, when she contributed "Solomon" to *Nymph Errant*. The critics raved.

No wonder this Manhattan-born diva came to call herself "One-song Welch." She might not have been a star, she told an interviewer recently, "but I was a name." After the success of *Nymph Errant* she found that London suited her and made it her home. There were enough musicals, stage revues, movies, and radio shows to keep her working at the top of the British entertainment world, without a thought of returning to the United States.

During World War II she traveled widely, performing for British forces in theaters of war from Gibraltar to Tobruk to Suez, in company with such stars of the British stage as John Gielgud, Beatrice Lillie, and Edith Evans. At home, meanwhile, her name assumed the status of legend, chiefly to those with long memories and large record collections. Finally, in 1980, she was invited to New York to appear in the musical retrospective *Black Broadway* and, predictably, created a sensation.

Throughout her career, Welch insisted that everything that had happened to her had been a matter of accident or coincidence. "Things that have happened in my life just happened," she told John S. Wilson of the *New York Times*. "I never had any star that I strove toward. . . . I've never made any effort to do anything. It's disgraceful."

LEE WILEY (1915–1975) is remembered now chiefly for her long association—and stylistic compatibility—with such jazzmen as cornetist Bobby Hackett, clarinetist Pee Wee Russell, pianist Joe Bushkin, and guitarist-raconteur Eddie Condon. But her smoky voice and languorous phrasing, coupled with a diction best described as "ladylike," won her wide admiration long before that. Arriving in New York as a teenager around 1930, she recorded with Leo Reisman and soon after began appearing with Paul Whiteman, Johnny Green and the Casa Loma Orchestra, and Victor Young, with whom she had a long professional and personal relationship.

The Oklahoma native became a fixture on radio during the 1930s and at decade's end made popular-music history by recording the first albums devoted exclusively to the works of single composers or collaborators, in this case Rodgers and Hart, George Gershwin, Harold Arlen, and Cole Porter.

Though her enunciation and delivery owed much to the influence of Ethel Waters, Lee Wiley had an elegance in her singing that was all her own and endeared her to such writers as the late Broadway historian Stanley Green ("I loved Lee Wiley even before I had any idea who she was") and critic-essayist George Frazier ("Miss Wiley has a little thing going for her called class. And class, I scarcely need remind you, is rare enough these days"). For Frazier, in fact, Lee Wiley was simply "one of the best vocalists who ever lived, with a magical empathy for fine old show tunes and good jazz." She left music in the middle 1940s, returning in the early 1970s for one final concert and record appearance.

JULIE WILSON (b. 1924) is the reigning queen of New York cabaret, admired—in some quarters nearly worshiped—for her magnetic, emotionally potent interpretations of classic pop material.

After taking an extended career sabbatical to raise two sons, she returned to performing in the mid-1980s. Her 1984 comeback show at Michael's Pub was, in fact, an all Cole Porter program; critics and audiences alike were taken with her interpretive insight and classic, high-style mystique. By the end of the following year she was a permanent fixture at the Oak Room of Manhattan's fashionable Algonquin Hotel, concentrating on Gershwin, Berlin, Arlen, Kurt Weill, and, of course, Porter.

Wilson first arrived in New York from her native Omaha in 1943, quickly progressing from chorus girl at the Latin Quarter to featured performer at the Copacabana, where she appeared with such stars as Tony Martin. Working in Miami Beach in 1947, she met Barron Polan, who became her manager (and the first of her three husbands) and booked her into the famed Mocambo in Los Angeles for her first solo singing engagement.

By the late 1940s Julie Wilson was a star. Even the visual image was firmly in place: skin-tight beaded gown on reed-thin body, hair pulled straight back in a bun, gardenia behind the ear. She originated the role of Bianca in the London production of Porter's *Kiss Me, Kate* in 1951 and shortly afterward starred as Nellie Forbush in *South Pacific*. Her Broadway highlights have included *The Pajama Game* and *Jimmy*.

Since her triumphant return to singing, Wilson has not had a moment to look back. She records regularly and performs often at New York's first-rank rooms. She has also appeared occasionally on the stage. Her portrayal of the indomitable Mme. Schuler in the 1990 off-Broadway production of *Hannah: 1939* was unforgettable. Two years earlier, at the Mark Hellinger, she played Flo, the nightclub owner with a heart of gold, in the short-lived *Legs Diamond*—and nearly saved the show.

"I feel it's miraculous that since I came back I haven't stopped working," she told *New York Times* critic Stephen Holden. "But I believe it's all fated. You just take it as it comes. The main thing is to keep going. I wouldn't dream of retirement. I never want to stop until I have to."

Performers

(First number refers to CD or cassette; the second to individual selection. For instance, 1:10 means CD/cassette 1, selection 10.)

Ambrose, Bert	*I've Got You on My Mind*	1:10
Andrews Sisters	*Don't Fence Me In* (w/Bing Crosby)	2:10
Armstrong, Louis	*You're the Top*	2:6
	Just One of Those Things	2:16
Astaire, Fred	*Night and Day*	1:12
	Please Don't Monkey with Broadway (w/George Murphy)	3:17
Bolcom, William	*The Physician* (w/Joan Morris)	1:19
Bowlly, Al	*In the Still of the Night*	3:6
Braff, Ruby	*Love for Sale* (w/Ellis Larkins)	1:6
Clooney, Rosemary	*It's Bad for Me* (w/Benny Goodman)	1:22
	Get Out of Town	3:13
Coleman, Emil	*I'm Getting Myself Ready for You*	1:1
Crosby, Bing	*Don't Fence Me In* (w/the Andrews Sisters)	2:10
Crosby, Bob	*I've Got My Eyes on You*	3:16
Cugat, Xavier	*Begin the Beguine*	2:12
Duncan, Todd	*River God*	3:10
Evans, Bill	*After You, Who?*	1:8
Fitzgerald, Ella	*Miss Otis Regrets*	2:8
	Do I Love You?	3:20
Forrest, Helen	*When Love Beckoned (on 52nd Street)* (w/Artie Shaw)	3:21
Freeman, Bud	*Just One of Those Things* (w/Bob Wilber)	2:17
Garland, Judy	*I Happen to Like New York*	1:4
	Easy to Love	2:19
	Friendship (w/Johnny Mercer)	3:19
Goodman, Benny	*It's Bad for Me* (w/Rosemary Clooney)	1:22
	Ridin' High	3:1
Holiday, Billie	*Night and Day*	1:13
Holman, Libby	*Love for Sale*	1:5
Horne, Lena	*At Long Last Love*	3:9
Kemp, Hal	*You're the Top* (w/Skinnay Ennis)	2:5
King, Teddi	*Where Have You Been?*	1:2
	I Concentrate on You	3:18
King, Tempo	*Swingin' the Jinx Away*	2:24
Larkins, Ellis	*Love for Sale* (w/Ruby Braff)	1:6
Lawrence, Gertrude	*Nymph Errant*	1:18
Lea, Barbara	*All through the Night* (w/Bucky Pizzarelli)	2:3
Martin, Mary	*Why Shouldn't I?*	2:15
	My Heart Belongs to Daddy	3:12
Martin, Tony	*Begin the Beguine*	2:11
Mercer, Johnny	*Friendship* (w/Judy Garland)	3:19
Mercer, Mabel	*Experiment*	1:16
	Ours	3:3
	It's De-lovely	3:4
Merman, Ethel	*I Get a Kick Out of You*	2:2
	Blow, Gabriel, Blow	2:4
	Down in the Depths (on the 90th Floor)	3:2

Mister Tram Associates	*Let's Step Out*	1:7
Morris, Joan	*The Physician* (w/William Bolcom)	1:19
Murphy, George	*Please Don't Monkey with Broadway* (w/Fred Astaire)	3:17
Nell, Edward, and the Foursome Quartet	*Don't Fence Me In*	2:9
Norman, Jessye	*In the Still of the Night*	3:7
Pierce, Hubbell	*What Am I to Do?*	3:15
Pizzarelli, Bucky	*All through the Night* (w/Barbara Lea)	2:3
Porter, Cole	*The Cocotte*	1:17
	Anything Goes	2:1
	When Love Comes Your Way	2:14
	Well, Did You Evah!	3:23
Reardon, Casper	*Easy to Love*	2:20
Roy, William	*Mister and Missus Fitch* (w/Julie Wilson)	1:11
Shaw, Artie	*Begin the Beguine*	2:13
	Rosalie	3:5
	I've a Strange New Rhythm in My Heart	3:8
	When Love Beckoned (on 52nd Street)	3:21
Short, Bobby	*How's Your Romance?*	1:15
	How Could We Be Wrong?	1:20
	Rap Tap on Wood	2:21
	Katie Went to Haiti	3:22
Siepi, Cesare	*I've Got You under My Skin*	2:23
Stewart, James	*Easy to Love*	2:18
Syms, Sylvia	*After You, Who?*	1:9
Tatum, Art	*Night and Day*	1:14
Waters, Ethel	*Miss Otis Regrets*	2:7
Welch, Elisabeth	*Solomon*	1:21
Wilber, Bob	*Just One of Those Things* (w/Bud Freeman)	2:17
Wiley, Lee	*Let's Fly Away*	1:3
	I've Got You under My Skin	2:22
Wilson, Julie	*Mister and Missus Fitch* (w/William Roy)	1:11
	Most Gentlemen Don't Like Love	3:14

Many additional artists appear on, but don't necessarily headline, these recordings. Among them are Bunny Berigan, Ray Browne, Joe Bushkin, Buck Clayton, Eddy Duchin, George Duvivier, Herb Ellis, Johnny Green, Urbie Green, Bob Haggart, Scott Hamilton, Dick Hyman, Harry James, Gene Krupa, Eddie Miller, Ray Noble, Tony Pastor, Oscar Peterson, Leo Reisman, Buddy Rich, Warren Vache, Jr., Cy Walter and Stan Freeman, John Williams and the Boston Pops, Lester Young, and Victor Young

Discography

Key to abbreviations

v vocal	ts tenor saxophone
c cornet	vn violin
flg flugelhorn	p piano
t trumpet	g guitar
tb trombone	sb string bass
cl clarinet	d drums
ss soprano saxophone	arr arranger
as alto saxophone	

* Indicates source recording is from the Yale Collection of Historical Sound Recordings

Compact Disc One/Cassette One, 1930–1934

THE NEW YORKERS (1930)

1. *I'm Getting Myself Ready for You*
Emil Coleman and his Orchestra

Recorded New York, c. 8 December 1930
Original 78 issue: Brunswick 6006*
Time: 2:36

Emil Coleman leading unidentified personnel, perhaps including Smith Ballew (v).

2. *Where Have You Been?*
Teddi King

Recorded New York, 1957
Original LP issue: *To You*, RCA Victor LPM 1313
Time: 3:07

Teddi King (v), with orchestra conducted by George Siravo and featuring Bernie Kaufman (as). Other personnel unknown.

3. *Let's Fly Away*
Lee Wiley

Recorded New York, 10 April 1940
Original 78 issue: Liberty L-296
Time: 2:50

Lee Wiley (v), with Bunny Berigan (t), Joe Bushkin (p), Sid Weiss (sb), George Wettling (d).

4. *I Happen to Like New York*
Judy Garland

Recorded London, 2–9 August 1960
Original LP issue: *Judy in London*, Capitol 94407
Time: 2:55

Judy Garland (v), with chorus and large studio orchestra conducted by Norrie Paramour. Personnel probably includes Kenny Baker, Stan Roderick (t); Don Lusher, George Chisholm (tb); Dave Lee (p); Kenny Clare (d).

5. *Love for Sale*
Libby Holman

Recorded New York, late January 1931
Original 78 issue: Brunswick 6045*
Time: 3:16

Libby Holman (v), with unidentified studio orchestra.

6. *Love for Sale*
Ruby Braff and Ellis Larkins

Recorded New York, 17 February 1955
Original LP issue: *Ruby Braff and Ellis Larkins*, Vanguard VRS 8019
Time: 5:35

Ruby Braff (t), Ellis Larkins (p).

7. *Let's Step Out* (added in 1930 to *Fifty Million Frenchmen*)
Mister Tram Associates

Recorded New York, 20 February 1988
Original CD issue: *Getting Some Fun Out of Life*, Audiophile DAPCD-241
Time: 2:14

Barbara Lea (v), Daryl Sherman (p/v), Dick Sudhalter (t/v), Loren Schoenberg (ts/v).

GAY DIVORCE (1932)

8. *After You, Who?*
Bill Evans

Recorded New York, April 1978
Original LP issue: *New Conversations—Monologue, Dialogue, Trialogue*, Warner Bros. M5 3177
Time: 3:35

Bill Evans (p).

9. *After You, Who?*
Sylvia Syms

Recorded New York, August–October 1989
Original CD issue: *... Then Along Came Bill, A Tribute to Bill Evans*, DRG 91402
Time: 3:25

Sylvia Syms (v), with Mike Renzi (p), Eddie Gomez (sb), Grady Tate (d).

10. *I've Got You on My Mind*
Ambrose and his Orchestra

Recorded London, 2 November 1933
Original 78 issue: Brunswick (England) 01623
Time: 2:31

Max Goldberg, Harry Owen (t); Ted Heath, Tony Thorpe (tb); Danny Polo, Sid Phillips, Joe Jeanette, Billy Amstell (reeds); Ernie Lewis, Reg Pursglove (vn); Bert Read (p); Joe Brannelly (g); Dick Ball (sb); Max Bacon (d); Sam Browne (v).

Side B (Cassette One)

11. *Mister and Missus Fitch*
Julie Wilson and William Roy

Recorded New York, 17, 24, 25 April 1989
Original CD issue: *Julie Wilson Sings the Cole Porter Songbook*, DRG SL 5208
Time: 1:57

Julie Wilson (v), William Roy (p/v).

12. *Night and Day*
Fred Astaire

Recorded New York, 22 November 1932
Original 78 issue: Victor 24193
Time: 3:26

Fred Astaire (v), with orchestra conducted by Leo Reisman and including Lew Conrad and Sammy Schklar (vn); Lew Sherwood (t); Ernie Gibbs (tb); Burt Williams and Jess Smith (reeds); Raymond Pugh (p). Other personnel unknown.

13. *Night and Day*
Billie Holiday

Recorded New York, 13 December 1939
Original 78 issue: Vocalian/Okeh OK 5377
Time: 2:55

Billie Holiday (v), with Buck Clayton, Harry Edison (t); Earle Warren, Jack Washington (as); Lester Young (ts); Joe Sullivan (p); Freddie Green (g); Walter Page (sb); Jo Jones (d).

14. *Night and Day*
Art Tatum

Recorded Hollywood, 21 January 1946
Original transcription: Armed Forces Radio Service (AFRS) P-545
Time: 1:27

Art Tatum (p).

15. *How's Your Romance?*
Bobby Short

Recorded New York, 17–22 July 1971
Original LP issue: *Bobby Short Loves Cole Porter*, Atlantic SD 2-606
Time: 2:21

Bobby Short (p/v), with Beverly Peer (sb) and Richard Sheridan (d).

NYMPH ERRANT (1933)

16. *Experiment*
Mabel Mercer

Recorded New York, 7 November 1954
Original LP issue: *Mabel Mercer Sings Cole Porter*, Atlantic 1213
Time: 3:15

Mabel Mercer (v), with Cy Walter, Stan Freeman (p), Frank Carroll (sb).

17. *The Cocotte*
Cole Porter

Recorded New York, 3 January 1935
Original 78 issue: Victor 24859*
Time: 2:42

Cole Porter (p/v).

18. *Nymph Errant*
Gertrude Lawrence

Recorded London, 18 October 1933
Original 78 issue: Victor 25226*
Time: 2:02

Gertrude Lawrence (v), with unidentified studio orchestra conducted by Ray Noble.

19. *The Physician*
Joan Morris and William Bolcom

Recorded New York, February 1988
Original CD issue: *Night and Day, The Cole Porter Album*, Omega OCD 3002
Time: 4:05

Joan Morris (v), William Bolcom (p).

20. *How Could We Be Wrong?*
Bobby Short

Recorded New York, 17–22 July 1971
Original LP issue: *Bobby Short Loves Cole Porter*, Atlantic SD 2-606
Time: 3:14

Bobby Short (p/v), with Beverly Peer (sb) and Richard Sheridan (d).

21. *Solomon*
Elisabeth Welch

Recorded London, 18 October 1933
Original 78 issue: Victor 25226*
Time: 3:08

Elisabeth Welch (v), with unidentified orchestra conducted by Ray Noble.

22. *It's Bad for Me*
Rosemary Clooney and the Benny Goodman Sextet

Recorded New York, 14 November 1955
Original 78 issue: Columbia 54293
Time: 2:54

Rosemary Clooney (v), with Benny Goodman (cl/v), Buck Clayton (t), Urbie Green (tb), Dick Hyman (p), Aaron Bell (sb), Bobby Donaldson (d).

Compact Disc Two/Cassette Two, 1934–1936

Anything Goes (1934)

1. *Anything Goes*
Cole Porter

Recorded New York, 27 November 1934
Original 78 issue: Victor 24825*
Time: 3:11

Cole Porter (p/v).

2. *I Get a Kick Out of You*
Ethel Merman

Recorded New York, 4 December 1934
Original 78 issue: Brunswick 7342*
Time: 3:04

Ethel Merman (v), with Johnny Green (p) and his Orchestra, probably including Angel Rattiner (t); Jimmy Lytell, Charles Dale, Ernest White, Murray Cohan (reeds); Leo Kruczck, Lou Kosloff, Joe Baum (vn); Perry Botkin (g); Kaspar Markowitz (sb); Al Lapin (d).

3. *All through the Night*
Barbara Lea, with Bucky Pizzarelli

Recorded Atlanta, 21 February 1989
Original CD issue: *You're the Cats!*, Audiophile ACD 252
Time: 3:23

Barbara Lea (v), Bucky Pizzarelli (g).

4. *Blow, Gabriel, Blow*
Ethel Merman

Recorded New York, 1 December 1947
Original 78 issue: Decca 24453
Time: 2:33

Ethel Merman (v), with the Foursome Quartet and orchestra conducted by Jay Blackton. Personnel unknown.

5. *You're the Top*
Hal Kemp and his Orchestra

Recorded New York, 14 December 1934
Original LP issue: *Hal Kemp and His Orchestra 1934*, Circle CLP-25 (transcription for World)
Time: 3:16

Earl Geiger, Russ Case (t); Gus Mayhew, Eddie Kusby (tb); Harold Dankers, Ben Williams, Saxie Dowell (reeds); John Scott Trotter (p/arr); Phil Fent (g); Jack Shirra (sb); Skinnay Ennis (d/v).

6. *You're the Top*
Louis Armstrong

Recorded Los Angeles, 15 August 1957
Original LP issue: *I've Got the World on a String*, Verve MGV 4035*
Time: 2:30

Louis Armstrong (v), with unidentified orchestra arranged and conducted by Russell Garcia.

Miscellaneous Song (1934)

7. *Miss Otis Regrets*
Ethel Waters

Recorded New York, 5 September 1934
Original 78 issue: Decca 140*
Time: 2:59

Ethel Waters (v), with unidentified studio orchestra possibly including Tommy Dorsey (tb) and Jimmy Dorsey (as/cl).

8. *Miss Otis Regrets*
Ella Fitzgerald

Recorded Los Angeles, 7 February 1956
Original LP issue: *Ella Fitzgerald: The Cole Porter Songbook*, Vol. 1, Verve V-4049

Time: 3:00

Ella Fitzgerald (v), Paul Smith (p).

Adios, Argentina (1934–35) (unproduced film)

9. *Don't Fence Me In*
Edward Nell and the Foursome Quartet
Cole Porter

Recorded New York, January 1935
Private recording, property of Cole Porter*
Time: 2:20 (includes speech and music)

Edward Nell with the Foursome Quartet (v), probably including Marshall Smith, Ray Johnson, Del Porter, and Dwight Snyder.

10. *Don't Fence Me In*
Bing Crosby and the Andrews Sisters

Recorded Los Angeles, 25 July 1944
Original 78 issue: Decca 23364*
Time: 2:59

Bing Crosby and the Andrews Sisters (v), with unidentified orchestra conducted by Vic Schoen. From the film *Hollywood Canteen*.

Jubilee (1935)

11. *Begin the Beguine*
Tony Martin

Recorded New York, 21 February 1954
Original LP issue: *Tony Martin Sings*, Dot ED 605
Time: 3:52

Tony Martin (v), with unidentified orchestra arranged and conducted by Henri René.

Side B (Cassette Two)

12. *Begin the Beguine*
Xavier Cugat and his Waldorf-Astoria Orchestra

Recorded New York, 5 September 1935
Original 78 issue: Victor 25133*
Time: 3:09

Xavier Cugat (vn), conducting unidentified personnel featuring Don Reid (v).

13. *Begin the Beguine*
Artie Shaw and his Orchestra

Recorded New York, 24 July 1938
Original 78 issue: Bluebird B-7764
Time: 3:15

Artie Shaw (cl), with Chuck Peterson, John Best, Claude Bowen (t); George Arus, Ted Vesely, Harry Rodgers (tb); Les Robinson, Hank Freeman (as); Tony Pastor, Ronnie Perry (ts); Les Burness (p); Al Avola (g); Sid Weiss (sb); Cliff Leeman (d).

14. *When Love Comes Your Way*
Cole Porter

Recorded New York, c. 1935
Private recording, property of Cole Porter*
Time: 1:38

Cole Porter (p/v).

15. *Why Shouldn't I?*
Mary Martin

Recorded New York, 25 January 1940
Original 78 issue: Decca 23148*
Time: 2:35

Mary Martin (v), with unidentified orchestra conducted by Ray Sinatra.

16. *Just One of Those Things*
Louis Armstrong

Recorded Chicago, 14 October 1957
Original LP issue: *Louis Armstrong Meets Oscar Peterson*, Verve MGV 8322
Time: 4:04

Louis Armstrong (t/v), with Oscar Peterson (p), Herb Ellis (g), Ray Brown (sb), Louis Bellson (d).

17. *Just One of Those Things*
Bud Freeman and Bob Wilber

Recorded New York, 10 and 12 December 1969
Original LP issue: *The Compleat Bud Freeman*, Monmouth-Evergreen 7022
Time: 3:46

Bud Freeman (ts), with Bob Wilber (ss), Ralph Sutton (p), Bob Haggart (sb), Gus Johnson (d).

Born to Dance (1936 film)

18. *Easy to Love*
James Stewart

Recorded Hollywood, 1936, for the film *Born to Dance*
Time: 1:08

James Stewart (v), with MGM studio orchestra, personnel unknown.

19. *Easy to Love*
Judy Garland

Recorded Hollywood, c. 1938, for the film *Love Finds Andy Hardy**
Time: 1:52

Judy Garland (v), with MGM studio orchestra, personnel unknown.

20. *Easy to Love*
Casper Reardon and his Orchestra

Recorded New York, 5 February 1940
Original 78 issue: Schirmer 511
Time: 3:03

Casper Reardon (harp), with Angel Rattiner (t); Alfie Evans, Milt Cassell, Henry Wade (reeds); Art Zazmar, Chauncey Morehouse (percussion); Loulie Jean Norman (v).

21. *Rap Tap on Wood*
Bobby Short

Recorded New York, 17-22 July 1971
Original LP issue: *Bobby Short Loves Cole Porter*, Atlantic SD 2-606
Time: 2:36

Bobby Short (p/v), with Beverly Peer (sb) and Richard Sheridan (d).

22. *I've Got You under My Skin*
Lee Wiley

Recorded Los Angeles, 10 February 1937
Original (12-inch) 78 issue: Decca 15034
Time: 2:18 (excerpt)

Lee Wiley (v), with Victor Young leading unidentified orchestra.

23. *I've Got You under My Skin*
Cesare Siepi

Recorded London, 1962
Original LP issue: *Bravo Siepi! The Broadway Songs of Cole Porter*, London 5705*
Time: 3:52

Cesare Siepi (v), with the Roland Shaw Orchestra, personnel unknown.

24. *Swingin' the Jinx Away*
Tempo King and his Kings of Tempo

Recorded New York, 15 October 1936
Original 78 issue: Bluebird B-6643
Time: 2:53

Tempo King (v), with Marty Marsala (c), Joe Marsala (cl), Queenie Ada Rubin (p), Eddie Condon (g), George Yorke (sb), Stan King (d).

Compact Disc Three/Cassette Three, 1936–1939

RED, HOT AND BLUE! (1936)

1. *Ridin' High*
Benny Goodman and his Orchestra

Recorded New York, 2 November 1937
Original LP issue: *1937–38 Jazz Concert No. 2*, Columbia ML 4613*
Time: 2:37

Benny Goodman (cl), with Harry James, Ziggy Elman, Chris Griffin (t); Red Ballard, Vernon Brown (tb); Hymie Schertzer, George Koenig (as); Art Rollini, Vido Musso (ts); Jess Stacy (p); Allan Reuss (g); Harry Goodman (sb); Gene Krupa (d).

2. *Down in the Depths (on the 90th Floor)*
Ethel Merman

Recorded New York, 6 November 1936
Original 78 issue: Liberty Music Shops L-206*
Time: 3:08

Ethel Merman with Fairchild and Carroll and their Orchestra, personnel unknown.

3. *Ours*
Mabel Mercer

Recorded New York, 7 November 1954
Original LP issue: *Mabel Mercer Sings Cole Porter*, Atlantic 1213
Time: 2:47

Mabel Mercer (v), with Cy Walter, Stan Freeman (p), Frank Carroll (sb).

4. *It's De-lovely*
Mabel Mercer

Recorded New York, 7 November 1954
Original LP issue: *Mabel Mercer Sings Cole Porter*, Atlantic 1213
Time: 3:39

Mabel Mercer (v), with Cy Walter, Stan Freeman (p), Frank Carroll (sb).

ROSALIE (1937 film)

5. *Rosalie*
Artie Shaw and his Orchestra

Recorded New York, 17 January 1939
Original 78 issue: Bluebird B-10126
Time: 2:46

Artie Shaw (cl), with Chuck Peterson, John Best, Bernie Privin (t); George Arus, Les Jenkins, Harry Rodgers (tb); Les Robinson, Hank Freeman (as); Tony Pastor, Georgie Auld (ts); Bob Kitsis (p); Al Avola (g); Sid Weiss (sb); Buddy Rich (d).

6. *In the Still of the Night*
Al Bowlly

Recorded London, 14 January 1938
Original 78 issue: HMV BD-502*
Time: 2:00 (excerpt)

Al Bowlly (v), with Ronnie Munro conducting the New Mayfair Orchestra, personnel unknown, but probably including Freddy Gardner (as).

7. *In the Still of the Night*
Jessye Norman

Recorded Boston, June 1984
Original LP issue: *Jessye Norman—With a Song in My Heart*, Philips Classics 412 625
Time: 2:40

Jessye Norman (v), with the Boston Pops conducted by John Williams.

8. *I've a Strange New Rhythm in My Heart*
"Art Shaw and His New Music"

Recorded New York, 17 September 1937
Original 78 issue: Brunswick 7971
Time: 2:44

Artie Shaw (cl), with John Best, Malcolm Crain, Tom di Carlo (t); George Arus, Harry Rodgers (tb); Les Robinson, Hank Freeman (as); Tony Pastor, Fred Petry (ts); Les Burness (p); Al Avola (g); Ben Ginsburg (sb); Cliff Leeman (d); Leo Watson (v).

You Never Know (1938)

9. *At Long Last Love*
Lena Horne

Recorded New York, 3, 5, 9, 13 June 1958
Original LP issue: *Give the Lady What She Wants*, RCA LPM LSP 1879
Time: 2:38

Lena Horne (v), with Lennie Hayton and his Orchestra, including Bernie Glow, James Maxwell, Al De Risi (t); William Byers, Vincent Forchetti, Frank Rehak, Eddie Bert (tb); Manny Gershman, Eddie Caine, Al Cohn, Romeo Penque, Danny Bank (reeds); Gene Di Novi (p); George Duvivier (b); Osie Johnson (d).

The Sun Never Sets (1938)

10. *River God*
Todd Duncan

Recorded London, 4 July 1938
Original 78 issue: Columbia (England) DB-1778*
Time: 3:10

Todd Duncan (v), with the Drury Lane Theatre Orchestra conducted by Charles Prentice, personnel unknown.

Leave It to Me (1938)

11. *My Heart Belongs to Daddy*
Mary Martin, interviewed by Pete Martin
Cole Porter, for the Tex and Jinx radio program

MM recorded 2 March 1960 (?); issued on the LP *Face to Face* (Decca DXD-166), a collection of interviews with Pete Martin for his series of articles in *The Saturday Evening Post* titled "I Call On . . ."*

CP recorded in New York, 1 December 1948 for the Tex McCrary and Jinx Falkenberg radio program*
Time (edited): 1:40

12. *My Heart Belongs to Daddy*
Mary Martin, with Eddy Duchin and his Orchestra

Recorded New York, 2 December 1938
Original 78 issue: Brunswick 8282
Time: 3:06

Mary Martin (v), with Eddy Duchin (p); A. Carroll or Lew Sherwood, Charles Trotta (t); unknown (tb); John Geller, Aaron Voloshin, Fred Morrow, Stanley Worth (reeds); Milt Shaw (vn); Horace Diaz (2nd p); Gene Baumgarden (g); Al Kunze (sb); Harry Campbell (d).

Side B (Cassette Three)

13. *Get Out of Town*
Rosemary Clooney

Recorded San Francisco, January 1982
Original LP issue: *Rosemary Clooney Sings the Music of Cole Porter*, Concord Jazz CJ-185
Time: 3:21

Rosemary Clooney (v), with Warren Vache (c/flg); Scott Hamilton (ts); David Ladd (fl); Nat Pierce (p); Cal Collins (g); Bob Maize (sb); Cal Tjader (vb); Jake Hanna (d).

14. *Most Gentlemen Don't Like Love*
Julie Wilson, with the Marshall Grant Trio

Recorded New York, 29 May 1957

Original LP issue: *Julie Wilson at the St. Regis*, Vik/ Victor LX-1118
Time: 2:12

Julie Wilson (v), with Marshall Grant (p), Mort Klanfer (sb), Jim Chapin (d).

THE MAN WHO CAME TO DINNER (1939)

15. *What Am I to Do?*
Hubbell Pierce

Recorded New York, 18–19 April 1973
Original LP issue: *Cole Porter Sung by Hubbell Pierce/Played by William Roy*, custom issue
Time: 2:11

Hubbell Pierce (v), with William Roy (p), Howard Collins (g), Paul Germano (sb), Jim Fitzsimon (d).

BROADWAY MELODY OF 1940 (film)
(Written in 1939)

16. *I've Got My Eyes on You*
Bob Crosby and his Orchestra

Recorded New York, 23 January 1940
Original 78 issue: Decca 2991
Time: 2:34

Max Herman, Billy Butterfield, Shorty Sherock (t); Warren Smith, Ray Conniff (tb); George Koenig, Bill Stegmeyer (as/cl); Eddie Miller, Gil Rodin (ts/cl); Irving Fazola (cl); Jess Stacy (p); Nappy Lamare (g); Bob Haggart (sb); Ray Bauduc (d); Marion Mann (v).

17. *Please Don't Monkey with Broadway*
Fred Astaire and George Murphy

Recorded Hollywood, 11 September 1939, for the sound track of the film *Broadway Melody of 1940*, MGM 25987*
Time: 3:28

Fred Astaire and George Murphy (v), with MGM Studio Orchestra, personnel unknown.

18. *I Concentrate on You*
Teddi King

Recorded Boston, c. 1953
Original LP issue: *'Round Midnight*, Storyville SLP 302
Time: 3:44

Teddi King (v), Beryl Booker (p).

DU BARRY WAS A LADY (1939)

19. *Friendship*
Judy Garland and Johnny Mercer

Recorded Los Angeles, 15 April 1940
Original LP issue: *Judy Garland from the Decca Vaults*, MCA 907 (previously unreleased take)
Time: 2:35

Judy Garland and Johnny Mercer (v), with unidentified orchestra conducted by Victor Young.

20. *Do I Love You?*
Ella Fitzgerald

Recorded Los Angeles, February 1956
Original LP issue: *Ella Fitzgerald: The Cole Porter Songbook*, Vol. 1, Verve 4049
Time: 3:48

Ella Fitzgerald (v), with unidentified studio orchestra conducted by Buddy Bregman.

21. *When Love Beckoned (on 52nd Street)*
Artie Shaw and his Orchestra
Helen Forrest, vocalist

Recorded New York, 9 November 1939
Original 78 issue: Bluebird B-10509*
Time: 3:13

Artie Shaw (cl), with Chuck Peterson, Harry Geller, Bernie Privin (t); George Arus, Les Jenkins, Harry Rodgers (tb); Les Robinson, Hank Freeman (as); Tony Pastor, Georgie Auld (ts); Bob Kitsis (p); Dave Barbour (g); Sid Weiss (sb); Buddy Rich (d); Helen Forrest (v).

22. *Katie Went to Haiti*
Bobby Short

Recorded New York, 17–22 July 1971
Original LP issue: *Bobby Short Loves Cole Porter*, Atlantic SD 2-606
Time: 4:38

Bobby Short (p/v), with Beverly Peer (sb) and Richard Sheridan (d).

23. *Well, Did You Evah!*
Cole Porter and cast of 1956 telecast

Recorded Los Angeles, 6 October 1956
Original issue: (from a telecast) T-2409
Time: 0:56

Cole Porter and Bing Crosby with unidentified personnel, in a broadcast tribute to Porter.

Bibliography

Balliett, Whitney. *American Singers*. New York: Oxford University Press, 1979.

Chilton, John. *Who's Who of Jazz: Storyville to Swing Street*. Philadelphia: Chilton Book Co., 1972.

Colin, Sid, and Tony Staveacre. *Al Bowlly*. London: Elm Tree Books, 1979.

Connor, D. Russell. *Benny Goodman: Listen to His Legacy*. Metuchen, N.J.: Scarecrow Press and the Institute of Jazz Studies, 1988.

Eells, George. *The Life That Late He Led: A Biography of Cole Porter*. New York: G. P. Putnam's Sons, 1967.

Ewen, David. *American Popular Songs from the Revolutionary War to the Present*. New York: Random House, 1966.

Fordin, Hugh. *The World of Entertainment: Hollywood's Greatest Musicals*. Garden City, N.Y.: Doubleday, 1975.

Fountain, Charles. *Another Man's Poison: The Life and Writings of Columnist George Frazier*. Chester, Conn.: Globe Pequot Press, 1984.

Grafton, David. *Red Hot and Rich!: An Oral History of Cole Porter*. New York: Stein and Day, 1987.

Green, Benny. *Let's Face the Music: The Golden Age of Popular Song*. London: Pavilion Books, 1989.

Green, Stanley. *Ring Bells! Sing Songs!: Broadway Musicals of the 1930s*. New Rochelle, N.Y.: Arlington House, 1971.

———. *The World of Musical Comedy: The Story of the American Stage as Told through the Careers of Its Foremost Composers and Lyricists*. New York: A. S. Barnes, 1960.

Hemming, Roy. *The Melody Lingers On: The Great Songwriters and Their Movie Musicals*. New York: Newmarket Press, 1986.

Hemming, Roy, and David Hajdu. *Discovering Great Singers of Classic Pop*. New York: Newmarket Press, 1991.

Hitchcock, H. Wiley, and Stanley Sadie. *The New Grove Dictionary of American Music*. London: Macmillan, 1986.

Kimball, Robert, ed. *Cole*. New York: Holt, Rinehart and Winston, 1971.

———. *The Complete Lyrics of Cole Porter*. New York: Alfred A. Knopf, 1983.

Kinkle, Roger D. *The Complete Encyclopedia of Popular Music and Jazz*. 4 vols. New Rochelle, N.Y.: Arlington House, 1974.

Lahr, John. *Notes on a Cowardly Lion: The Biography of Bert Lahr*. New York: Alfred A. Knopf, 1969.

Larkin, Philip. *Required Writing: Miscellaneous Pieces, 1955–1982*. New York: Farrar, Straus and Giroux, 1984.

Laubich, Arnold, and Ray Spencer. *Art Tatum: A Guide to His Recorded Music*. Metuchen, N.J.: Scarecrow Press, 1982.

Mattfeld, Julius. *Variety Music Cavalcade 1620–1961: A Chronology of Vocal and Instrumental Music Popular in the United States*. Englewood Cliffs, N.J.: Prentice-Hall, 1962.

Merman, Ethel, with George Eells. *Merman*. New York: Simon and Schuster, 1978.

Pleasants, Henry. *The Great American Popular Singers*. London: Victor Gollancz, 1974.

Raben, Erik, ed. *Jazz Records, 1942–80: A Discography*. Vols. 1/2. Copenhagen: Jazz Media, 1989.

Rust, Brian A. L. *The American Dance Band Discography 1917–1942*. 2 vols. New Rochelle, N.Y.: Arlington House, 1975.

———. *The Complete Entertainment Discography, from the Mid-1890s to 1942*. New Rochelle, N.Y.: Arlington House, 1973.

———. *Jazz Records, 1897–1942*. 2 vols. New Rochelle, N.Y.: Arlington House, 1978.

Schuller, Gunther. *The Swing Era: Development of Jazz, 1930–1945*. New York: Oxford University Press, 1989.

Schwartz, Charles. *Cole Porter: A Biography*. New York: Dial Press, 1977.

Shaw, Artie. *The Trouble with Cinderella: An Outline of Identity*. New York: Farrar, Straus and Young, 1952.

Simon, George T. *The Big Bands*. 4th ed. New York: Schirmer; London: Collier Macmillan, 1981.

Simon, George T., et al. *The Best of the Music Makers*. Garden City, N.Y.: Doubleday, 1979.

Terkel, Studs. *Hard Times: An Oral History of the Great Depression*. New York: Pantheon Books, 1970.

Whitburn, Joel. *Pop Memories—1890–1954*. Menomonee Falls, Wis.: Record Research, Inc., 1986.

Whiting, Margaret, with Will Holt. *It Might As Well Be Spring: A Musical Autobiography*. New York: William Morrow and Co., 1987.

Wilder, Alec. *American Popular Song: The Great Innovators, 1900–1950*. New York: Oxford University Press, 1972.

Credits

Executive Producer: Raymond L. Shoemaker, Indiana Historical Society
Producers: Susan Elliott, Robert Kimball, Richard M. Sudhalter
Technical Coordination: Malcolm Addey
Transfers: John R. T. Davies, Richard Warren, Jr.
Discs supplied by: John R. T. Davies, Alexander Garvin, Ron Jewson, Robert Kimball, Arthur Siegel, Daryl Sherman, Richard M. Sudhalter, Yale University Library
Booklet Editors: Susan Elliott; Paula Corpuz, Indiana Historical Society
Project Designer: Tony Woodward, Indiana Historical Society

PHOTO CREDITS:

Culver Pictures: 32 top, 59 bottom, 60, 64 bottom, 67 top, 79 top and bottom right, 82, 85 top, 88
Eileen Darby: 12 top
Frank Driggs Collection: 16, 18, 20, 23 bottom, 26 bottom, 31 bottom, 34 bottom, 38, 41 top, 42 top, 54, 64 top, 70, 76, 79 bottom left, 80, 87 top, 93 top and right
The Helen Forrest Collection/Coward, McCann & Geoghegan: 67 bottom
The Mabel Mercer Foundation: 87 bottom
Miami County, Indiana, Historical Society: opposite page 1, 3 bottom left, 11 bottom, 14
Museum of Modern Art/Film Stills Archive: 47 top
The Cole Porter Musical and Literary Property Trusts: 3 top, 4, 6, 8, 11 top, 12 bottom, 23 top, 26 top, 31 top, 32 bottom, 41 bottom, 47 bottom, 73
Christian Steiner/Philips Classics Productions: 93 bottom left
Van Damm Photos, The New York Public Library, Astor, Lenox and Tilden Foundations: 34 top, 42 bottom, 52, 57, 59 top
Yale University Library: 3 bottom right, 50

SPECIAL ACKNOWLEDGMENTS:

Many of the recordings used in this compilation were Cole Porter's own, which he bequeathed to Yale University. They are now part of the Yale Collection of Historical Sound Recordings, which furnished this project with many other recordings as well. "You're the Top: Cole Porter in the 1930s" would not have been possible without the valuable guidance and assistance of Richard Warren, Jr., curator of the Yale Collection of Historical Sound Recordings.

The producers also wish to extend special thanks to the Cole Porter family: Margaret Cole Richards, Ralph Richards, James Cole, and Alice Cole; to The Cole Porter Musical and Literary Property Trusts, Robert H. Montgomery, Jr., Trustee, F. Richard Pappas, and Florence Leeds, Executive Secretary; to Warner Chappell Music, Inc., Les Bider, Chairman and Chief Executive Officer, Jay Morgenstern, Executive Vice President and General Manager, and Frank Military, Senior Vice President; to Cathedral Arts, Inc., Thomas J. Beczkiewicz, Executive Director, and Lewis C. Ricci, Director of Special Projects; and to John Leffler of John Leffler Associates.

Finally, the producers extend special thanks to Robert Altshuler, Edmund Anderson, Jean Bach, Charles Bourgeois, Ruby Braff, Susan Davies, John De Vries, Wendell Echols, George Eells, Chris Ellis, John McLellan Fitch, Hugh Fordin, Alexander Garvin, Daphne Hellman, Roy Hemming, Dick Hyman, Ron Jewson, Bernie Kaufman, Helen Keane, Bonnie Lake, Burton Lane, Barbara Lea, David Lee, Tom MacCluskey, John Meyer, Dan Morgenstern, Joe Muranyi, William Roy, Artie Shaw, Daryl Sherman, Bobby Short, Arthur Siegel, George T. Simon, Sylvia Syms, John S. Wilson, Julie Wilson, and Jeff Zaraya.

The producers acknowledge the serious omission of Frank Sinatra from this collection. They were unable to obtain permission to use any of his Cole Porter recordings, specifically his 1956 interpretation of "At Long Last Love" with the Nelson Riddle Orchestra; "Just One of Those Things," from the 1954 film *Young at Heart*; and "Well, Did You Evah!," which he recorded with Bing Crosby in 1956 for the film *High Society*.

The Producers

Susan Elliott has worked in a wide variety of musical genres as a writer, composer, pianist, and producer. Her composing skills have been applied to commercial jingles and several children's books and recordings. The chief classical music critic for the *New York Post*, Elliott is currently a music journalist and a consultant to the Opera Musical Theater program of the National Endowment for the Arts. She has served as managing editor of *High Fidelity*, music textbook editor for Holt, Rinehart and Winston, and public affairs director for RCA (now called BMG) Records.

Robert Kimball is a music theater historian and an authority on Cole Porter, the Gershwins, Irving Berlin, Richard Rodgers and Lorenz Hart, Noble Sissle, and Eubie Blake. He is also artistic advisor to the Ira Gershwin estate and to The Cole Porter Musical and Literary Property Trusts. Kimball was responsible for the 1982 Secaucus, New Jersey, discovery of thousands of scores and manuscripts by Kern, the Gershwins, Porter, and many more. The former curator of the Yale Collection of the Literature of the American Musical Theatre, Kimball is currently editing "The Complete Lyrics of Ira Gershwin." Other books include *Cole*, *The Complete Lyrics of Cole Porter*, *Reminiscing with Sissle and Blake*, and *The Gershwins*.

Richard M. Sudhalter is a jazz cornetist, author, producer, music historian, and critic. A popular recording artist and featured player, leader, and musical director of major concerts and jazz festivals, Sudhalter is known for his re-creations of the Paul Whiteman Orchestra of the late 1920s, with himself as soloist. A Grammy-winning record sleeve annotator, Sudhalter is principal author of the authoritative Beiderbecke biography, *Bix: Man and Legend*, and is currently at work on a jazz history for Oxford University Press. Additionally he has been a jazz critic for the *New York Post* and is artistic director for jazz at New York's Vineyard Theatre.

A Word from the Producers

If the assembly and production of this collection of songs Cole Porter wrote in the 1930s has taught us any lesson, it is this: consensus is a goal often blithely conceived, cheerfully sought, and only arduously and painfully attained. In other words, when the subject is music, people have a tough time agreeing.

Work on this collection began in the fall of 1990, when the three of us met in Yale University's Historical Sound Recordings archive under the benevolent eye of curator Richard Warren, Jr. As the acknowledged Porter authority, Bob Kimball had come primed with a list of songs he thought should be considered and some notes on recordings he knew to be in the Yale collection.

As we began the process of auditioning, it quickly became clear that all of us had strong, clearly defined ideas about Porter's songs and about how they should be sung and played. Kimball is a man of the musical theater, Dick Sudhalter a player and chronicler of jazz and its varied traditions; Susan Elliott moves with equal ease through classic pop and the concert hall. Each of us was eager to defend his and her pet partisanships.

In view of this, our one ground rule should come as no surprise: nothing accepted on faith. Any recorded interpretation that seemed even marginally enticing to one of us got a hearing. In some cases, we spent hours of listening time to find a version that rang bells for all three. Kimball mined his seemingly bottomless stack of show albums. Sudhalter spent long hours taping obscure jazz records, a couple of which are represented. Warren came up with a few surprises of his own. At a conservative estimate, we collectively listened to about 150 recorded hours of Porter songs.

Sometimes the going was tough. And sometimes—as in Bobby Short's masterful reading of "How Could We Be Wrong," or the late-night alchemy wrought by Teddi King with "I Concentrate on You"—it was remarkably easy. So many Porter songs were strong enough to support multiple versions. It is astonishing, for example, to hear what contrasting moods, colors, and musical implications emerge from "Night and Day," as interpreted by Fred Astaire and Billie Holiday.

Passions rose and passions fell, as drama high and low was played out around the conference table. In the end good sense prevailed, compromise supplanted partisanship, and consensus walked sweetly and softly among us. We are all quite pleased with the results and about what this collection shows about the richness and variety of Cole Porter's music. And that, after all, is what the whole exercise has been about.

The Yale Collection of Historical Sound Recordings

Richard Warren, Jr., Curator

Established in 1961 as a department of the Yale University Libraries, the Yale Collection of Historical Sound Recordings (HSR) collects, preserves, and makes available for study important historical recordings in the fields of Western classical music, jazz, American musical theater, drama, literature, and history. It owes its existence to Mr. and Mrs. Laurence C. Witten II, whose comprehensive collection of early vocal recordings, donated at HSR's inception, is generally considered the finest of its kind in the world.

A large number of individual and corporate donors, as well as a selective acquisitions policy, have in subsequent years increased HSR's holdings in other areas as well. Most recordings have been collected because they represent performers important in their own right; also collected extensively are recordings in which a composer was personally involved, Cole Porter being a prime example.

HSR also incorporates the American Musical Theatre Collection, which contains scores, manuscripts, books, recordings, and memorabilia. Founded in 1953 by the late Robert Barlow, whose personal holdings form its basic material, the AMTC includes the archives of Cole Porter (Yale 1913), Harold Rome (Yale 1929), and E. Y. Harburg, among others, as well as major collections from Irving Berlin, Noble Sissle, and Eubie Blake.

Today some 120,000 recordings reside at the HSR, approximately 90 percent of which are discs, two-thirds of these being pre-LP recordings. The remaining 10 percent includes reel-to-reel tapes, along with some cassette tapes and cylinders.

In addition, HSR maintains a large library of printed materials and microfilms, which provide historical, biographical, and discographical support information.

Open to faculty members and students of Yale, HSR is also available, by appointment, to serious researchers outside the University. Historical Sound Recordings/Yale University Library/P. O. Box 1603A Yale Station/New Haven, CT 06520.